CASE STUDIES OF THE CLINICAL INTERPRETATION OF THE BENDER GESTALT TEST

CASE STUDIES OF THE CLINICAL INTERPRETATION OF THE BENDER GESTALT TEST

Illustrations of the Interpretive Process
for Graduate Training and
Continuing Professional Education

By

CLIFFORD M. DeCATO, Ph.D.

Assistant Professor
Acting Director of Graduate
Education in Psychology
Hahnemann Medical College and Hospital
Philadelphia, Pennsylvania

and

ROBERT J. WICKS, M.A.

Doctor of Psychology Program
Hahnemann Medical College and Hospital
Philadelphia, Pennsylvania

With a Foreword by

Zygmunt A. Piotrowski, Ph.D.

Professor of Psychiatry (in Psychology), Retired
Thomas Jefferson University
Adjunct Professor of Psychology
Temple University
Philadelphia, Pennsylvania

CHARLES C THOMAS • PUBLISHER
Springfield • *Illinois* • *U.S.A.*

Published and Distributed Throughout the World by

CHARLES C THOMAS • PUBLISHER

Bannerstone House

301-327 East Lawrence Avenue, Springfield, Illinois, U.S.A.

With THOMAS BOOKS *careful attention is given to all details of
manufacturing and design. It is the Publisher's desire to present books that are
satisfactory as to their physical qualities and artistic possibilities and
appropriate for their particular use.* THOMAS BOOKS *will be true to those
laws of quality that assure a good name and good will.*

Printed in the United States of America
R-1

Library of Congress Cataloging in Publication Data

DeCato, Clifford M
    Case studies of the clinical interpretation of
the Bender gestalt.

    Bibliography: p.
    Includes index.
    1. Bender gestalt test--Case studies.
I. Wicks, Robert J., joint author. II. Title.
[DNLM: 1. Bender-Gestalt test--Case studies.
2. Psychology--Education--Case studies. WM145
D291c]
BF698.8.B4D4   155.2′84   75-46640
ISBN 0-398-03554-7

TO OUR FAMILIES

FOREWORD

COPYING of geometric designs of moderate complexity is a task which nearly all human subjects, especially adults, can master easily. Only relatively minor variations in performance occur with time in normal subjects. Marked changes in performance have been found to correlate positively with marked personality changes. Thus the test is sensitive to conspicuous personality changes which, as a rule, are pathological. The test is sensitive also to the subject's enduring personality traits. Deviant test findings suggest a deviant personality, but the reverse is frequently not true. Sometimes, an insidious illness leaves the test performance almost intact or modified so little that it takes fine discrimination and wide experience to detect the change and to interpret its specific significance. The reasons for changes in performance are manifold and not necessarily mutually exclusive.

Regular repetition of the same performance under the same conditions implies order; and there is no order without a meaningful system. To illustrate the main outline of such a system, the authors offer a number of individual case studies. These studies will help the students to understand what type of information can be obtained with the aid of the test, regardless of psychiatric or neurological diagnoses. The process of deducting the personality traits is independent of the knowledge of diagnosis. In their presentation of the cases, the authors concentrate on principles of interpretation of test findings which have the best chance of passing the test of time. Their conclusions are unequivocal and capable of a validity check by past or future clinical observations. This collection of individual case studies will doubtless prove to be a very valuable teaching aid.

Zygmunt A. Piotrowski

ACKNOWLEDGMENTS

MANY people contributed directly or indirectly to the development of a book, and we wish to express our warmest thanks to all who have helped make this work possible.

Foremost among the persons who have contributed by their support and encouragement have been our wives, Kathy DeCato and Michaele Wicks. Without them this book would never have been a reality.

To Drs. Zygmunt Piotrowski and Jorge Montero we wish to express our appreciation for their comments and support. Many students have also contributed through their stimulation, questioning and interest. Among the students who have been most actively involved through contact in supervision or spontaneous personal interest have been Linda Valentini, Sarita Shapiro, Allan Pfeffer, Leslie Stein, Arlene Stofflet, Deena Adler and Ken Byrne.

We wish to acknowledge the stimulation afforded by Hahnemann Medical College and Hospital. Participation in the Mental Health Sciences Department, under the direction of Dr. Israel Zwerling, provided a general impetus to this work. Ms. Cheryl Haufler provided excellent clerical and typing work in preparing the manuscript, and for this we cannot thank her enough.

Finally, the authors wish to express their gratitude to Dr. Lauretta Bender and the American Orthopsychiatric Association for permission granted to use Plate 1 and Plate 62 from the monograph, *A Visual Motor Gestalt Test and Its Clinical Use* (Plates A-1 and A-2).

C.M.D. & R.J.W.

CONTENTS

CASE STUDIES OF THE CLINICAL INTERPRETATION OF THE BENDER GESTALT TEST

"All that a man does is physiognomical of him. You may see how a man would fight by the way in which he sings; his courage, or want of courage, is visible in the word he utters, in the opinion he has formed, no less than in the stroke he strikes. He is one; and preaches the same self abroad in all these ways."*

*From *Sartor Resartus and On Heroes and Hero-Worship*, by Thomas Carlyle. An Everyman's Library Edition. Published in the United States by F. P. Dutton & Co., Inc., and reprinted with their permission. All rights reserved.

Chapter 1

INTRODUCTION

Background and Purpose

THE present work grew out of the training and supervisory interests of the primary author. Relatively few works are available that present a view of the strategy and thinking a clinician uses in analyzing a Bender Gestalt protocol as part of a diagnostic psychological test battery. Accordingly, the authors believed that a casebook of BVMGT analysis would be very helpful to novice clinicians as they learn to use this technique of personality assessment.

The primary purpose of this book then is to serve as an introduction to the BVMGT as a technique for assessing personality dynamics, developmental level and psychopathology. As is more clearly explained in the interpretation section, clinical inferences incorporate data from many sources, not the least of which is the clinician's own experience. This work does not offer new theories or formulate new hypotheses. The purpose of these case analyses is to demonstrate how the complex, often intuitive thinking of the clinician unfolds as he studies a person's Bender reproductions and incorporates understandings derived from many sources. Observing the process used by a person familiar with a technique can be a helpful adjunct in acquiring clinical skills.

No suggestion is intended that the method presented here is the only approach or the most suitable technique for every clinician. Rather, the purpose of these studies is to illustrate one clinical method which is offered as a general guide for persons who wish to develop their skills in Bender Gestalt interpretation. Ultimately each clinician must develop his own style of interpretation in which he integrates his own experience with other sources of knowledge.

Brief Literature Review

Since the appearance of the original basic work by Lauretta

Bender (1938), the BVMGT became widely integrated into diagnostic psychological testing as a technique for visual-motor, developmental and personality assessment. A critical or exhaustive review of the literature is beyond the scope or intent of the present volume.

A review by Tolor and Schulberg (1963) revealed the existence of over 300 research and clinical works related to the BVMGT. A search of the *Psychological Abstracts* from 1967 to present yielded over eighty-five studies and reports involving the Bender Gestalt technique. Our purpose in mentioning this cursory review is to draw the reader's attention to the fact that a large body of clinical and research data on the BVMGT has accumulated. This body of literature provides a general background for the clinician interested in deepening his knowledge about the nature of the BVMGT as a clinical instrument.

For our purposes we particularly recommend certain works as basic readings for the type of interpretation illustrated in the present case studies. These works are fully listed in the references — Lauretta Bender, *A Visual Motor Gestalt Test and its Clinical Use*, 1938; Edna A. Lerner, *The Projective Use of the Bender Gestalt*, 1972; Max L. Hutt, *The Hutt Adaptation of the Bender Gestalt Test*, 1969; Elizabeth M. Koppitz, *The Bender Gestalt Test with the Human Figure Drawing Test for Young School Children*, 1972; and Aileen Clawson, *The Bender Visual Motor Gestalt Test for Children*, 1962.

Sample of Cases

BVMGT protocols were selected to give samples of child and adult reproductions and to show a variety of features frequently encountered in clinical work. Cases were drawn from a wide variety of settings ranging from inpatient and outpatient clinics for children and adults to special schools for children with learning disabilities and private practice.

To insure the anonymity of all records only case numbers were used once a record was selected for interpretation, and no detailed clinical data or facts about the person were included that could in any way lead to the person's identification.

This procedure somewhat reduced the specificity of supporting clinical data for inferences but was felt necessary to insure confidentiality. Of course, the direct inferences drawn from the protocols were in no way limited and clearly allowed a presentation of the manner in which inferences can be obtained from the BVMGT. Enough general clinical information was retained to give some idea about those hypotheses which proved strongest. The "Integration" section of each case analysis represents the inferences which appeared to have the most clinical support.

Method of Administration

The technique used to administer the Bender Gestalt for the cases studied in this book involves elements common to clinical diagnostic testing. The equipment used was a set of BVMGT cards produced by Western Psychological Services, eight and one-half inch by eleven inch white typing paper, a smooth surface that the person could sit up to and reach comfortably such as a desk or table, and lead pencils usually of about a number 2 softness.

Uniform instructions were used in administering the Bender to each patient. This particular set of instructions incorporates common clinical practices which have been refined through experience. The instructions assume the individual has already been introduced to the purposes of the testing and has been prepared for the variety of tasks he/she is about to do. The person is then told,

> *Now I am going to show you some simple line drawings, one at a time. There are nine designs here. I want you to copy them as best as you can.*

Clawson (1962) proposes a slightly different formula for children. Hutt (1969) discusses administrative techniques at considerable length. A single sheet of paper is placed in front of the person with the long side perpendicular to the person. Each card is then placed one at a time at the top of the paper lying flat on the table. If the person turns the paper sideways, the examiner turns the paper back and says, *Please leave it like this.* Similarly, if the person turns the stimulus card, the examiner turns it back and asks the individual to leave it in its proper orientation. If the person attempts to turn the paper sideways a second time, the examiner notes this in his record of the Bender performance but does not correct it a second time.

The examiner keeps a detailed record of statements the individual makes, counting, direction of drawing and the amount of time taken to execute the reproductions. With experience, clinicians develop a feel for about how much time it takes the average person to copy the Bender drawings. Studies and clinical experience suggest that about ten minutes is the average. Individuals who go beyond fifteen minutes in copying the drawings or who copy the drawings in less than five minutes may be revealing any of a number of traits and dynamics which have clinical significance.

When the individual has completed all the drawings, the stimulus cards are removed and the page of drawings is placed out of the individual's sight. Then the examiner says, *Now I would like you to draw as many of the designs as you can from memory,* again handing the individual a single sheet of paper. In the recall phase of the Bender the examiner again notes in detail how the subject draws and the sequence of the recall of each reproduction as well as comments by the person about his own work.

The literature describes other elaborations on this basic technique. One such method is to obtain the person's associations to each design. Another variation is to have the person redraw all the designs in any way he wishes. These variations require an increase in the length of time needed to administer the diagnostic battery. For this reason the present work used only BVMGT reproductions and recall records administered in the fashion described above. Hutt (1969) and Lerner (1972) discuss the other techniques in considerable detail.

Method of Interpretation

The clinician in actual practice will ordinarily approach a case with some form of basic organization to his analytic efforts, yet still maintain a general flexibility in the variety of hypotheses he maintains. For example, in one case the most outstanding feature of the record may be the high degree of disorganization. In this instance the clinician may ponder about the disorganization present and study this aspect of the Bender record in much more detail than some of the other factors which he might study in other cases. In every case, however, there is some form of general overview of the figures which yields a general impression. An overview is often signaled by such statements as "What strikes me the most about this record" or "the outstanding thing here" or "in general" and so on in the case analysis.

Every analysis covers certain basic aspects of the reproductions and will usually include line pressure, quality of Gestalt, direction and sequence, organization, figure size, work methods and use of space. While these and other dimensions are common to every BVMGT reproduction, the individuality of the person emerges from the quality, degree and pattern of successes and failures in reproducing the designs. Koppitz (1972) and others have developed and researched scoring systems which can aid in determining the probable significance of various types of errors in relation to the age of the individual. Whether or not a specific scoring system is systematically applied, the basic data from such research becomes part of the clinician's frame of reference in formulating hypotheses (inferences) from the BVMGT.

In seeking a means to illustrate the process of analysis, the authors developed a general schemata to improve organization and communication of the Bender Gestalt interpretations. The first stage of the analysis involves gaining an overview, a general impression or Gestalt of the person from the most salient and outstanding features of the copy phase. The next step is a more detailed analysis of specific features. This is immediately followed by an examination of each figure individually for its possible symbolic significance.

The analysis of the copy phase is followed by a similar analysis of the recall phase with a change in emphasis. In the recall analysis major attention is placed on a comparison between the copy and the recall. The general basis for the difference in interpretation between copy and recall is explained in Adult Case 01.

Once the basic analysis of both copy and recall is achieved, the clinician must attempt to sort out which hypotheses have the most support and are the most likely. Once this is done an initial statement is formed about the person's functioning. The "Integration" section of each case analysis is the place where the clinician synthesizes a view of the person from the inferences which appear to have received the most support. At this point the authors also take time to draw more abstract inferences about personality, dynamics, psychopathology and possible organicity. Some general information from other clinical data is often also included in the section to give a flavor of the relevance that the inferences have to the entire diagnostic and treatment situation.

The "Comment" at the end of each case, is, on the one hand, designed to point out features of the analysis which are of particular interest in the given case and, on the other, a brief exposition illustrating or explaining various aspects and principles involved in the technique.

A theoretical discussion of the nature of the inferential process is beyond the scope of this book. Schafer (1954) has a detailed discussion of projective testing and the adequacy of inferences from the Rorschach which in many respects appears valid for the Bender Gestalt. Hutt (1969) has a number of chapters addressed to psychodiagnosis and the inferential process specifically related to Bender Gestalt. However, some general comment in this volume on the nature of inferences may be helpful to the novice in keeping a perspective.

Clinical interpretation is a mixture of science, art and technology. The scientific aspect of this enterprise is contributed by the research literature which yields a network of information about what the given test measures and provides a comparison between the given person and others who have been tested with the Bender Gestalt. Clinical experience and literature similarly provide a data base for the inferential process. The technological aspect comes from a relatively standardized mode of administration and recording as well as the application of specific scoring criteria. The art involves the observational and creative powers of the individual clinician in both the administration phase and the interpretation phase of the technique by which he shapes and integrates a complex view of the individual's personality and functioning.

Single responses are seldom an adequate basis for drawing a final conclusion about whether a person has a given trait, personality trend or psychopathology. In actual clinical practice the Bender Gestalt is seldom used alone except as a gross screening device. As part of a battery of tests which often includes techniques ranging from the Wechsler Intelligence scales to the projective tests (Thematic Apperception Test, figure drawings, Rorschach and many other tests from which the clinician may select a battery), the Bender Gestalt provides a rich source of information for generating hypotheses about a person. Whether these inferences ultimately are retained depends on data from other sources in the battery or from general clinical data available on the person. To illustrate the concept of interpretation of the Bender Gestalt in a test battery we have made references to where we might seek evidence from other tests in the battery in the course of our interpretations. References to types of test data beyond the Bender Gestalt that would help clarify various inferences should be regarded as helpful leads for the specific case, not as the only possible way to confirm or clarify the given hypothesis.

In the final analysis it is the individual clinician who must generate the inferences, select among the myriad possibilities and synthesize a coherent, practically useful picture of the person. The clinician's own personality and cognitive style combine with his training and experience to create the final product, a group of interrelated concepts and observations about a person which aids in understanding and managing the treatment process.

Interpretation of Children's BVMGT
As Compared to Adult BVMGT

The general principles of interpretation briefly discussed in the previous section apply to both child and adult records. Inferences are developed out of general knowledge and clinical experience which reveal the meaning of various types of performance on the Bender Gestalt. Whether the reproductions are those of children or adults the Bender reproductions primarily provide a measure of the individual's visual motor functioning at the time he/she executed the designs as that functioning is experienced by and is an expression of the whole person.

Beyond the general principles, however, the significance of various performances is often very different for children than for adults. For example, four out of five children use an eraser (Clawson, 1962), and it becomes significant if a child does not use an eraser. By contrast, most adults do not erase and erasures become interpretable in the more mature age ranges. Similarly, many features of children's records show various types of characteristics (pencil pressure, organization, integration, angulation, etc.) which would be interpretable for adults but which primarily reflect the general level of visual-motor maturation for children.

In brief, normative expectations for children are not the same as for adults and must be known for adequate interpretation of a child's record (See Clawson, 1962, and Koppitz, 1972). Moreover, in general children change very rapidly whereas adults tend to change much more slowly. The "Literature Review" section includes a list of works which are especially useful in acquiring information about the Bender Gestalt with children and adults.

A brief overview of the general trends in visual-motor development, leading to a mature level of functioning as seen in Bender Gestalt reproductions, is given here to provide a frame of reference for the case interpretations.

Certain basic principles tend to apply in general. First, as the child increases in mental age, the drawing responses tend to become more articulated, more clearly discriminated and reveal a better retention of form (Gestalt). The productions become more accurate copies of the stimulus drawings, reflecting a clearer development in conceptual capacity, visual imagery and fine motor coordination. Second, as the child increases in age there is a tendency for him/her to be able to conceptualize a greater number of parts and relate these parts of a task or of an object to each other in a complex fashion. This capacity is revealed in the Bender by the presence of increasing degrees of organization. The first stage of such organization is the placing of any drawing on a page and remaining within the structure of the edges of the page.

Clinical experience and developmental research indicate that, on an average, a child of approximately three years of age can contain his drawings on a page without going off the edge (DiLeo, 1973). The next stage of organization is reflected by an ability to place figures on a page with space around them.

Between the ages of six and eight the individual's capacity for calibrating the distance from one figure to another as he begins the drawing becomes sufficiently accurate so that he can reproduce a design without colliding with another design. During this stage of the development of drawing organization, the individual may or may not show evidence of forming a sequence of the figures. That is, the individual may choose to place the designs on the page more by space availability than by some form of conceptual plan as to the order in which the figures will be drawn.

The final stages of development in the drawing organization occur when the individual reveals some form of order and sequence in the drawing such as from left to right or from top to bottom. In mature individuals who have relatively well-developed visual-motor coordination and personality features related to organization, the record contains not only figures reproduced accurately and with some logical sequence but also a capacity for varying to some degree, i.e. left to right sequence interrupted once by the person in order to go in a somewhat different direction. Such a level of organization is expected to develop some time during adolescence. The exact time this development is attained in adolescence is influenced by many factors including mental age, sociocultural influences and personality trait formations and dynamics.

In terms of the specific figures, the capacity for drawing circular figures preceeds the capacity for drawing figures with angles. It is common knowledge in clinical work and child development that the circle developmentally preceeds the square which developmentally preceeds the diamond. In other words the motions and imagery that are required and the degree of calibration of visual-motor coordination that is necessary to produce a circle are less demanding than for figures requiring angles. As rough developmental norms, the circle occurs at approximately two to three years of age and evolves out of a general scribble. Angles appear sometime thereafter, with five years of age being about average for the construction of a square. The oblique angles of the diamond are most difficult and do not tend to be achieved by the average child until approximately seven and a half years of age.

The final basic developmental consideration of the Bender involves integration of separate figures. The capacity to draw single figures preceeds the capacity to integrate the figures accurately. For example, the capacity to draw both a circle and a square is usually achieved around five years of age. However, the capacity to accurately integrate a circle touched by a square, as in Design A on the Bender, is generally not achieved until some time between the ages of six and eight.

The capacity to reproduce all of the designs of the Bender Gestalt showing good form level and flexible organized sequence tends to occur some place between the ages of nine and eleven (Koppitz, 1972; Clawson, 1962). Clawson (1962), presents plates of Bender protocols taken from normal children from ages seven through eleven and also presents numerous records of children with histories of emotional and/or neurological disturbances if the reader wishes to see samples of both types of records.

By way of summary, the clinical use of the Bender Gestalt has a foundation in normal human development and factors that influence visual-motor coordination and personality integration. Deviations from expectancy have been correlated with a variety of factors, any of which can interfere with the individual's capacity for perceptual motor functioning and may vary from low intellectual capacity to personality disorganization or decompensation such as that seen in psychotic disorders. Central nervous system dysfunction which impairs inhibition, integration and other ego-level capacities can also interfere in an individual's ability to carry out the task of copying or recalling the Bender designs at an age-appropriate level. Sociocultural factors are among the variables that can also affect the rate of development.

While all of these factors are also considerations in the clinical use of the Bender Gestalt with adults, they are essential to the interpretation of records with children. What is an appropriate level of integration, coordination and perceptual motor functioning for a four-year-old may be a deficient level for an older child and vice versa. Without an understanding of the normal expectancies associated with maturation, mental age and personality development, interpretations run a high risk of being grossly invalid for the individual.

In the analyses and discussion of all of the cases in the present work, the foregoing principles and foundation knowledge in psychological testing are assumed and are the basis on which interpretations are made, whether or not the principles are explicitly stated in the analyses of any given individual record. An effort was made to explain the derivation of many of the hypotheses in the cases. In order to avoid excessive repetition and to allow the flavor of the interpretative process to emerge, however, explanations were often omitted. The works listed in the "Literature Review" and the "Bibliography" provide a basis from which the interpretations may be more clearly understood.

Organization and Use of This Work

This book is divided into a section of adult cases and a section of child cases. No attempt has been made to supply a thorough exposition of basic theoretical or background information on the Bender Gestalt in this volume or with each case since that has been amply done in other works. However, in certain instances where it was deemed helpful, references to these other works were noted during interpretations of specific protocols.

The reader will probably gain the most from this work by undertaking a thorough preliminary reading of the entire work and then later returning to those records that are similar to protocols he/she is analyzing for further study. Readings in the recommended literature (see section on literature review) should also prove helpful in understanding the basis of many of the inferences. Ideally, this method will help demonstrate both the similarities in method of analysis from one case to another while showing how the unique, idiosyncratic patterns and styles of a personality can be extracted from the Bender productions.

Cautionary Notes: The Limits of Inference

As with all diagnostic clinical testing, the clinician needs careful scholastic and supervised practical training in order to learn the actual process of making inferences from psychological techniques. This casebook obviously cannot substitute in any way for the thorough clinical and didactic training needed to actually apply and use psychological testing as diagnostic tools. Specific inferences need to be understood in the light of what can be hypothesized and what cannot be inferred from any given test, what has been found valuable and useful in clinical experience, and what is of a more tentative or speculative nature.

The authors wish to sound a word of caution about the nature of interpretations given to the sample cases. The purpose of these case studies is to illustrate a process, not to imply that these inferences are the only possible conclusions. Since the interpretive process involves knowledge from clinical experience as well as research, interpretations can change as the clinician learns new correlates to Bender performance from clinical work or new research emerges modifying the understanding of what the Bender Gestalt measures.

Diagnostic testing is a dynamic process involving a creative act on the part of the clinician as well as scientific information. At the moment an inference is made there is often a deceptive aura of finality which can easily lead an observer to feel that the clinician believes there is one and only one possible inference. The true state of affairs is quite otherwise. Many possible correlates of performance on the Bender Gestalt exist. The task for the clinician is not simply to draw an inference of the type (X signifies Y, [X=Y] where X stands for a Bender reproduction and Y stands for a personality trait, developmental level or pathology), but to sort out which hypotheses have the highest likelihood when it is understood that X can sometimes signify Y while understanding it may also signify some other set of factors. Clinical interpretation in this work is regarded as a highly complex process in which there is no substitute for the clinician's own experience and creative processes, tempered by training and data available from research.

Chapter 2

INTERPRETATION OF
ADULT PROTOCOLS

CASE: 01

AGE: 32

SEX: Female

Analysis of Copy Phase

WHAT initially impresses us about this record is the high degree of conflict that is reflected in both the way she cramped the figures together in the middle of the page and simultaneously varied the size of individual figures (some were smaller than the stimulus designs and some were significantly larger and more expansive). This pattern suggests inner turmoil and emotional conflicts which she struggles to contain as seen in the constrictedness of spacing but which sometimes gets out of hand and are acted out as seen in the more expansive designs which collide with others, e.g. Figure 7 collides with Figure 6. Unevenness in size is associated as well with difficulties in modulation of emotions and impulses. Ordinarily we would check this hypothesis against the reaction to color on the Rorschach to gain further evidence of how she integrates her emotions and cognition.

By the time the average person reaches midlatency age (around 8 years) he/she can organize the designs on the page with space separating them. When collisions occur in records of adults, a severe degree of disturbance is often manifested. At the very least, collision shows that there is usually strong interpersonal hostility and disregard for boundaries between objects which clinically often reveal themselves in interpersonal conflicts. Central nervous system impairments and mental deficiency can be involved in collisions. A differential diagnosis from the Bender alone can only be regarded as highly tentative.

15

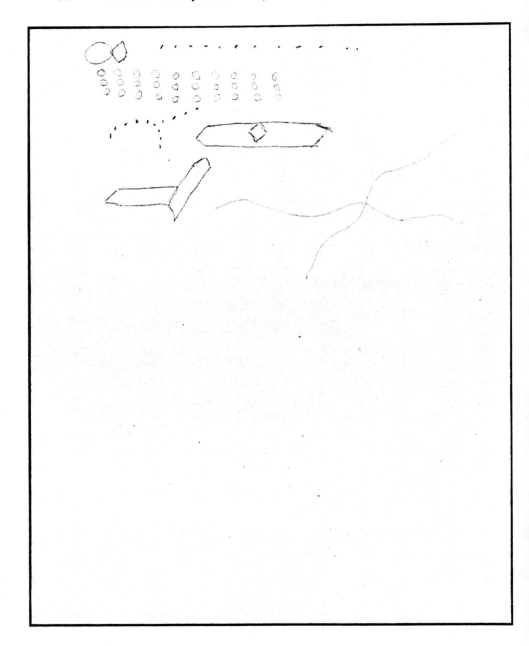

Case 01, Adult ~~Copy~~ *Recall*

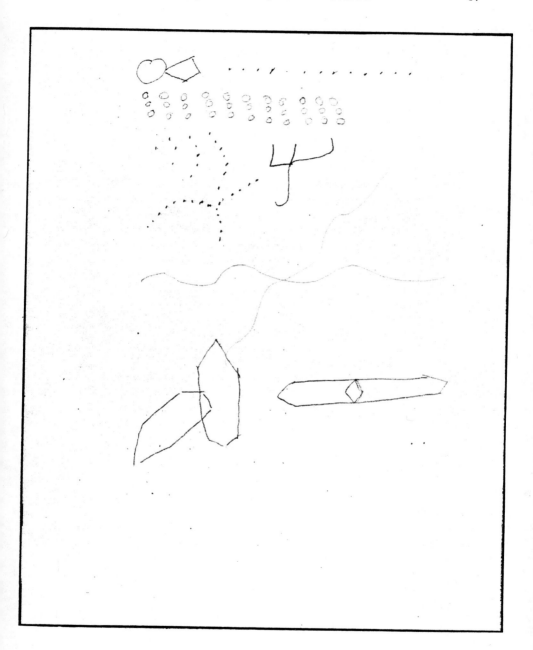

Case 01, Adult ~~Recall~~ *copy*

In the present instance other signs of organicity (difficulties with Gestalt, angulation errors, rotations, line quality) are either absent or minimal. This suggests that functional and personality variables are the more likely determinants of the collision. The relatively high number of designs recalled suggests at least an average intelligence, minimizing the chances that retardation is involved. Analysis of the Wechsler Intelligence Scale as well as other indices would help determine the final differential diagnosis in this regard.

Regardless of etiology, collisions indicate that the person does not always use good judgment and forethought. In an adult such a severe degree of impairment in judgment reflects disturbances in ego level functions and indicates a more severe psychopathological condition, possibly of a psychotic or borderline psychotic quality. Other clinical information in the present case confirmed the hypothesis of severe emotional disturbance and interpersonal difficulties resulting from strong hostile-dependent trends in her personality.

The way in which a person executes the specific designs can be a rich source of information about perceptual-motor functioning and personality. Both the graphological aspects (quality of Gestalt, line quality, pressure of pencil on page) and the symbolic-associative value of each design play a part in the clinician's analysis of individual designs. It should be noted that the hypotheses generated by the symbolic aspect of the designs are regarded as highly speculative. Although we have found such inferences to be accurate in many cases, we tend to regard them primarily as a means of generating ideas whose confirmations must come from other aspects of the Bender and other sources in the full test battery. If such evidence is lacking, these hypotheses must be regarded as extremely tenuous.

These cautions, whether stated or not, should always be kept in mind, especially when attempting symbolic interpretations. In the remainder of the book such cautionary notes will often be omitted in order to reduce repetitiveness. The reader should remain aware, nevertheless, that the symbolic hypotheses from specific designs have been interpreted with full awareness of the tentative nature of such hypotheses and the ever constant need to seek further verifications within the test battery or with the aid of other general knowledge (interview data, clinical history, direct observations, etc.).

Turning next to interpretations based on individual designs, we noticed that some distortion occurs in Figure A. The size is diminished and the square subpart is elongated. Since this is the first design it suggests she approaches a new task with anxiety and possibly apprehension about her ability to perform well and that she constricts as a means of coping with her anxiety. The relationship between the two subparts is slightly distorted, suggesting she has more than average problems in interpersonal relations, quite possibly around concerns about male-female relationships. At any rate, information about her sexual identity formation and her interpersonal adjustment should be sought from the test material and interviews since we are alerted to potential problems in this area from Figure A.

Figure 1 reveals a continued regressive trend toward distortions. The Gestalt is maintained showing that her defenses and capacity for reality level functioning do work to an extent. At the same time, there are slight distortions. Some dots are converted to slashes or squiggles, and an extra dot is added reflecting a slight tendency toward perseveration. These distortions suggest underlying conflict and struggles to contain angry or hostile feelings very likely generated in part by the demand of the task for concentrated, goal-directed effort. There is a brittleness in her defenses. Her impulses seem to break through in spite of her efforts to contain them.

Designs 2 and 3 are essentially intact and reflect a capacity to recover from anxiety-produced regressions and at least at times function at a relatively effective reality level. Design 3 does show some tendency to begin to expand, and increasing tension is revealed in the formation of the dots as she progressed from left to right.

Design 4 has two important distortions — a decrease in the size and a flattening tendency in the curved subpart. There is also a slight concave given to the left vertical line of the open square subpart. These distortions after two relatively well-executed designs make us wonder if something about Design 4 did not arouse anxiety-provoking images, fantasies or associations.

This design has often been interpreted as two objects with oral implications (the rectangle touching the curve is thought to resemble something touching a breast, i.e. nurturing or oral dependency imagery). The distortions suggest she may have unresolved conflicts around getting her emotional needs met. This hypothesis was strengthened by clinical observations that she was very dependent and demanding in her behavior.

Skipping Designs 5 and 6 temporarily, Design 7 is thought to have symbolic value for dependency hypotheses. One subpart of Figure 7 is vertical and appears to support the other subpart which is leaning against the vertical. This design is thought to have symbolic implications for feelings and associations about dependency. Since the design is drawn so much larger than most of the designs there is further suggestion to compliment Design 4 that dependency is an area that is of particular concern for this person. Shakiness in the line quality and lack of closure at the intersection of angles suggests poor personality integration under the impact of anxiety.

Design 8 which has one large figure containing a smaller figure is also thought to have implications for feelings about dependency relationships. The prototype of close, intimate dependency is the mother-child relationship and derivations from conceptions of this relationship to others in later life. The smaller subpart of Figure 8 reveals sketching which is usually associated with anxiety and uncertainty of some type and further enhances the general hypothesis that she experiences difficulty and concern beyond average around her dependency relationships.

Returning to Design 5, the general Gestalt is retained and the same phenomena as were seen in Designs 1 and 3 again appear — that is, while essentially correctly executing the design as she progresses in the task, there are signs of increased tension in the pressure in the dots and changes in form of the dots. These types of change tend to be associated with efforts at control of impulses and suggest chronic emotional conflict and low frustration tolerance. Her controls rather quickly give way under stress, indicating a fragile personality structure.

Design 6 has two major distortions. First, the size is larger than the stimulus design, and second, both horizontal and vertical subparts are simplified, i.e. some of the sine waves are omitted. Following a general pattern of constriction up to this point the sudden increase in expansiveness is marked. This trend toward expansiveness continues through Design 7, suggesting that her efforts at self-control and frustration tolerance in doing the task are beginning to give way, and she is yielding more to impulse with a concomitant decrease in her adaptation. The simplification in Design 6, when considered in the light of the other trends discussed, tends to indicate that at times she carries out a task with insufficient attention to details and in a hasty and incomplete fashion. Analysis of the way she approached the area components of the Rorschach, especially the level at which she tends to analyze and integrate the percepts as well as analysis of her use of form components, would help deepen and clarify this last hypothesis.

Analysis of Recall

Before beginning the analysis of the recall phase of this first record the authors would like to briefly indicate certain basic assumptions and postulates that underlie the analysis of the Bender recall. An extensive review is beyond the scope of the present work and the reader is referred to the "Bibliography" for other sources that examine the basic theoretical and empirical postulates of Bender interpretation.

The recall places persons much more on their own than the copy phase. They must rely on their own visual-motor capacities as well as on capacities for memory, storage and retrieval of images, information and associations. They must organize the order of recall and execution of designs without the structured guidance of the stimulus cards. It has often been observed that individuals tend to experience this part of the task as the most stressful. Frequently people will comment about their feelings of inadequacy and occasionally may refuse to attempt the task, offer rationalizations and engage in other defensive and compensatory maneuvers. The recall, because it does place a person on his/her own so much, affords rich information about personality structure, defenses, interpersonal attitudes, memory, intelligence and areas of conflict that can complement or conflict with the way the person functions in the more guided and structured copy phase.

The same basic principles of interpretation for the copy phase apply for the recall with a slightly different emphasis. In analyzing the recall the emphasis is more on the reactions of persons to being left on their own. One major underlying assumption of recall analysis is that if the individual has a relatively mature level of personality and cognitive development, there should be no significant changes other than in the number and order of designs from the copy to the recall.

In other words, it is assumed that the individual would function relatively evenly in executing the specific designs unless there are interferences brought about by developmental deficiencies, internal conflicts and/or areas of personality or cognitive weakness effected by the demand characteristics of the recall phase. Significant changes in the designs on the recall as compared to the copy are interpreted as reflecting the impact of the stress of the situation and the personal attributes of the individual.

Two aspects of this woman's recall are striking. First, the tendency to constrict seen in the copy is more obvious. The designs are generally smaller in size, cramped together and hug the top of the page. When left on her own, her anxiety apparently increases, and she attempts to cope by shrinking back from an open field and sticking close to the edge which helps her organize herself and feel more secure. Clinically, this type of pattern is usually the mark of timid and fearful persons who do not trust their own adequacy and do not like to be independent or be in situations demanding responsibility, initiative and decisiveness. This general inference was amply born out by extended observations of this person who exhibited a clinging, helpless quality in her interpersonal relations.

The second striking feature is reflected in the trend that can be found in the distortions. While in general, inferences made in the copy phase for designs 1, 5 and 8 still hold, there were important changes in designs A, 6 and 7. The changes in A and 7 point to difficulties in interpersonal relations — that is, problems around the point of contact between objects. The overall trend toward an increase in distortions indicates that under the stress of being left on her own her judgment becomes poorer and her adaptation becomes less dependable and flexible. Finally, as noted previously, she recalled seven designs which is somewhat above average (average adult recalls about four to six designs), which suggests that her intelligence is probably at least in the average range. The errors observed are not likely to have been the product of mental deficiency. This means other factors, i.e. personality development, conflicts, are more apt to be the determinants of the observed patterns of strengths and weaknesses than intelligence per se.

Integration

Before proceeding with the integration of Case 01, we wish to make some comments on the purpose of the "Integration" section in these case studies.

The general goal of the "Integration" section of the analysis is to achieve a view of how the whole person functions and where the individual is strong or weak. Achieving such a synthesis requires that the psychologist identify and abstract those themes and inferences which receive the most confirmation and which have the highest probability of indicating valid personality trends and constructs.

From the patterns of levels of functioning along the various dimensions measured by the Bender, a picture of the individual's current personality functioning emerges. It is from this constellation of integrated inferences that implications for psychopathology or treatment management can be fashioned. In this final integration as in all aspects of the analysis it must be kept in mind that the understanding achieved from the Bender alone is at best incomplete and needs elaboration from other sources before being retained as final.

This woman presents the picure of a person with much poorly-modulated inner conflict and strong hostile-dependency trends which would be expected to cause strain in her interpersonal relations. She often displays very poor judgment and forethought resulting in sporadic acting out of her impulses with insufficient regard to reality boundaries and the impact of her actions on others.

She experiences chronic high levels of anxiety in part generated by conflicts around expressing or containing her angry and aggressive feelings and in part related to strong feelings of inadequacy and low self-esteem. She attempts to control her anxiety by constricting her actions and avoiding situations where she would have to take responsibility or act decisively. These defensive maneuvers only partially achieve their goals. At times she acts in an overly constricted fashion while at other times she suddenly becomes inappropriately assertive and expansive.

It should be noted in regard to these hypotheses that one reason for her referral for testing was because in a therapeutic situation it was felt that she should be able to function in a less dependent and more mature fashion, and her erratic behavior puzzled the therapists. In the light of the Bender analysis it seems that the erratic behavior is clearly related to severe conflicts and anxiety with strong hostile dependency as a major personality component. Moreover, the Bender also indicated average or better intelligence. The combination of erratic, conflict-ridden infantile behavior in an obviously intelligent person made her unpredictable and puzzling as she could not really live up to her intellectual potentials for any length of time. Yet, for *short* periods of time (as seen in the Bender protocol) she could function at a level commensurate with her age and intelligence.

The severity of the anxiety and the personality constriction, the erratic and brittle quality of the defenses, and the strong infantile dependency trends in a person this age suggest a relatively severe disorder, one most apt to be encountered in psychotic or borderline psychotic disorders and at the very least involving deficiencies in ego development. A final differential diagnosis would depend on other testing and clinical information. Many strengths are manifested by this person and should be recognized in determining the course of treatment. She appears to have at least average intelligence and responds with increased effectiveness when in a guided, structured situation. Although she appears to have strong interpersonal conflicts, she can at times use good judgment and integrate herself with her environment in an adaptive manner.

Comment

This first Bender protocol reveals most of the basic features of Bender analysis with adults. Certain dimensions of Bender records have through research and clinical experience been shown capable of revealing aspects of personality structure and functioning. The way in which the person approaches, reacts to and copes with the examiner, the demands of the testing situation, and the stimulus designs are paralleled by his interactions in his life, his internal emotional states and his efficiency in using his resources to cope and adapt. In analyzing a Bender record the clinician is seeking to understand the intricate and subtle relationships between a whole living person and his environment.

In this search for understanding, certain dimensions of the Bender are examined in nearly every analysis. These dimensions include the graphology (pressure on page, line quality, accuracy of Gestalt), organization, use of space, method and approach in working, and symbolic implications. These dimensions are related to prior experience in the field, research, normative data on development and relationships to personality constructs and psychopathology. The individuality and uniqueness of each person emerges from the patterns of strengths and weaknesses in structure and function emerging from the analysis of the protocol. All persons share capacities for various modes of perceiving and reacting to internal and external stimuli. The way in which persons integrate their emotions, cognition and perception, however, is unique and is revealed in both their manner of approach to the task and efficiency in carrying out the complex functions involved. Personal styles emerge, revealing trends and themes unique to that person as well as those which are shared with the majority of people.

In the final integration the clinician abstracts those themes and hypotheses that receive the greatest degree of confirmation. The view of the personality and cognitive emotional functioning that emerges is considered only tentative. Final retention or rejection of a view of the person is attained only through supplemental data from other cognitive and projective devices in the test battery. In those instances where the Bender is administered as the sole technique, the analysis can be considered only as a screening device to generate ideas, associations and hypotheses to help the psychologist gain some general tentative understanding of the person. When used in this way it can also provide leads for further diagnostic work and management of the treatment program.

CASE: 02

AGE: 30

SEX: Female

Analysis of Copy

Many of the features that stand out in this record collectively suggest rigidity, high anxiety and ego-level deficiencies. The extreme reduction in size of all the figures implies a strong constriction and shrinking back from contact with others. The way her drawings hug the paper's edge is further evidence of fear of venturing out to others in the world.

She spontaneously numbered the figures; this is usually associated with intellectual defenses such as isolation of affect, compartmentalization and obsessive-compulsive defense mechanisms. The numbering reflects an attempt to handle anxiety by being precise. Yet the quality of the Gestalt of the figures reveals many distortions, suggesting that her defenses are failing and that unacceptable impulses or ideation are breaking through despite her efforts at control. In the same vein, the numbering further suggests she seeks and feels a need for external structure to integrate herself.

Line quality provides added support for postulating the presence of a diffuse disorder. The pressure on the page is extremely light which reflects low energy. Withdrawal and depression are among the factors which can lead to such light pressure. Line quality also reveals some shakiness which can be associated with either anxiety or central nervous system dysfunction.

Compound figures are separated showing joining problems

Case 02, Adult Copy

Case 02, Adult Recall

(Figs. A, 4 and 7). Impairments in perception as well as strong interpersonal anxieties and withdrawal can underlie such distortions. There are many problems with angulation. At this point the line quality, separations and angulation distortions clearly imply that her capacity for accurately perceiving, for concentrated sustained effort, and for control over fine motor coordination are markedly impaired.

A final differential diagnosis is not possible from her Bender reproductions alone since the features so far described can be produced by either central nervous system dysfunction or severe functional personality conflicts. Clinical observation, however, did confirm a high degree of anxiety, withdrawal, depression and rigidity in her personality and sufficient impairment in her interpersonal and reality level functioning to require temporary hospitalization.

Analysis of the individual figures can often reveal subtleties and nuances of personality that go beyond the general inferences derived from the overall analysis.

Figure A reveals numerous distortions and errors. The shrinkage in size has already been noted and is characteristic of all her reproductions which means that this feature of her personality is general rather than associated with the specific symbolism of any given figure. For this reason size will not be analyzed any further in the interpretation of specific designs.

The most striking feature of Design A is the separation suggesting she has difficulty imaging and conceptualizing complex Gestalts. She may have conflicts around integrating objects in general, a hypothesis that receives strong confirmation from Figures 4 and 7. Object relations are very likely impaired. Her ability to give and receive support and affection is markedly reduced.

Persons showing such withdrawal have usually experienced traumatic object relations during their developmental years, leaving them with expectations of hurt and disappointment from others which they defend against by withdrawal, denial and projection. There is usually also a history of moderate to severe emotional deprivation leaving the person with chronic feelings of rage toward nurturing persons. A detailed history from the patient and from informants (family, relatives, etc.) would help clarify these inferences. Data from the TAT and Rorschach would also provide further information about her conception of object relations and would help clarify her defensive patterns.

The shaky line quality in Design A is a general feature of her functioning and therefore may have no specific significance in relation to this figure. The circle is somewhat smaller and more distorted than the square, suggesting she may have feelings of inferiority around her conception of femininity. Her sexual identity is very likely to be one source of conflict for her and should be carefully explored in the House-Tree-Person, the TAT and the Rorschach. Given her general alienation and anxiety around themes of object relations, it is likely that her male-female relationships are also a source of anxiety and conflict for her.

Figure 1 shows minor distortions. She adds one dot which is not enough to be considered a perseveration but does suggest she is not precise in her reality perceptions and contacts even though she makes a display of precision by numbering all the designs. The dots are converted to tiny dashes suggesting highly controlled underlying feelings of anger and conflict around aggressive impulses. Turning dots to dashes was perseverated within Designs 1, 2, 3 and 5. This type of perseveration is often associated with functional disorders where the person is struggling to control angry feelings and aggressive impulses. Some mild unevenness in line quality suggests her controls are not working smoothly and some decompensation is threatening.

Figure 2 is simplified, first by turning the circles into dashes and second by omitting some columns of circles. She has poor frustration tolerance with a tendency to give up easily, take the simple way out, and not finish goals she undertakes. Unevenness is seen in the horizontal plane with mild rotation first counterclockwise, then clockwise. Similar unevenness in the horizontal plane is observed in Figures 1 and 3, suggesting that she is struggling against depression. She starts out with an upward (counterclockwise) rotation and ends with a downward (clockwise) swing. This characteristic implies she at first tries to resist her depressive feelings but soon fatigues and begins to succumb to the depression. Further evidence of depression should be sought in the content of the TAT and in numerous features of the Rorschach (long reaction times, dark shading, depressive content and other indices).

The simplification of dots to dashes in Figure 3 has already received comment as has the clockwise rotation. One other distortion not yet discussed is the uneven spacing of the dots reflecting breaks in her functioning. The angulation has been blunted and flattened, suggesting she has anxiety around her aggressive impulses which sometimes interferes with her smooth functioning. She tries to control by flattening her affect.

Figure 4 shows problems of mild rotation and lack of closure in the joining of the subparts which has been interpreted previously. The only additional inference specific to Design 4 is the distortion of the curved subpart, suggesting there are conflicts in this woman around acceptance of her oral dependent needs. Schizoid persons often have difficulty in joining the breast-like curve to the rectangular figures which together with the other separations is strong evidence that this woman has severe problems in making contact with other people.

Figure 5 shows distortion in the base of the figure which is elongated and in the phallic-like projection which is elongated and slightly rotated clockwise. These distortions suggest discomfort around imagery and associations of masculinity. She may overexaggerate the power of the male and yet simultaneously put males down or see them as impotent. Together with Figure A this is evidence she has some specific conflicts around her sexual identity and male-female relationships.

Figure 6 has numerous distortions. The vertical subpart is grossly distorted with the Gestalt of sinusoidal lines being partially lost. The horizontal line is cramped and the curves have increased angulation. Altogether these distortions suggest she has uneven emotional expression which at times becomes confused, interrupted and chaotic. This figure also suggests she has much conflict around accepting her own emotions and integrating her emotions with cognition. Analysis of the way she copes with color in the Rorschach would help understand the degree to which her emotions interfere with her reality testing.

The separations in Figure 8 have been discussed. The size differential implies she feels small, and the lack of connection suggests she has serious difficulties in giving or receiving in her interpersonal relations which was also noted in Figure 4. The loss of angles may be part of her tendency to simplify tasks; this could involve either a neurological substrate or personality characteristics. The cutting off of angles is sometimes seen with suicidal persons.

Figure 8 shows a further loss of angulation and a distortion of the Gestalt. Since she was able to reproduce the angles of Figure A fairly well, the increased difficulty with angles seen in Figures 7 and 8 may well be associated with fatigue from concentrated effort. The adequacy of her controls and reality testing appears to be slipping. If so, there is reason to suggest she is verging on personality decompensation since the average person has sufficient stamina and mental control to sustain them throughout the Bender without impact on reality level adaptation. Persons who show this degree of fatigability, conflict, rigidity and impairment psychotic decompensation or have diffuse organic dysfunction.

Analysis of Recall

She recalled an average number of figures, suggesting her intellectual function falls in the average range. The placement against the margin, numbering and shrinkage in size have the same implications that were discussed in the copy phase.

The Gestalt shows further deterioration with all the figures recalled showing some simplification, suggesting that when she must rely on her own resources she is less adequate than in a structured situation. Her memory trace tends, at times, to be quite unreliable.

Figure 5 has fewer dots than the stimulus and has a slight clockwise rotation again showing a tendency toward flattening of affect and depression. The design she labeled "2" could have come from either the stimulus Figure 7 or Figure 8 and shows loss of angles and tremulous line quality. The difficulty in identifying which stimulus figure gave rise to this memory reproduction is a measure of the degree of inefficiency. It also indicates that there is a regression of her ego level functioning when she is left on her own.

Figure 6 is very small suggesting strong inhibition, constriction and repression of affect, resulting in a pronounced tendency to flatten emotional expression. Figure 2 shows three distortions. First, she simplified the design by omitting most of the rows of circles. Second, the circles were converted to dots and, third, an extra row of dots was added. She distorts memory traces, elaborates on her memories and alters reality to suit herself, all of which suggest regression in reality testing and judgment. She began to produce a fifth design by first numbering, then could not recall the figures which suggests she is to some degree aware of her own memory deficiency and that structure doesn't always help her to deal with anxiety.

Integration

This woman presents the picture of a person who is very withdrawn, fearful of contact with people and highly anxious about interacting closely with others. Object relations are marked by anxiety and an inability to give or receive support in close interdependent relationships.

Much inhibition, repression of affect and depression are evident. She is fearful of experiencing or expressing spontaneous affect or feeling intense emotion. She attempts to overcontrol feelings and interpersonal interactions by rigid adherence to orderliness and a variety of intellectual defenses which are only suggested and not fully defined by her Bender reproductions. The price of such extreme overcontrol is inhibited emotional spontaneity.

Her defenses are brittle and fragile with generally regressed and deficient reality level adaptation. She is unable to sustain extended efforts at concentration, imagining and fine motor coordination. Fatigue soon begins to reduce her tenuous adjustment and further erodes her capacity for reality level adaptation. When she is left on her own her resources prove even more depleted, suggesting that her capacity for problem solving in daily life is very likely to be regressive and inefficient.

By way of summary, this woman resembles persons who have ego-level impairments with long-standing chronic deficiencies in object relations and emotional control and expression. Her affect is flat and overcontrolled, and her resources for realistic problem solving are depleted and constricted with indications of anxiety and depression of mood. This degree of overcontrol and ego deficiency is most likely to be found in the more severe forms of psychopathology, especially the psychoses or the borderline psychoses and/or intracranial disorders. The other cognitive and projective tests and general clinical information would help establish a final differential diagnosis.

Comment

The Bender reproductions given by this woman afford an opportunity to see how long-standing personality trends and components (inhibition, overcontrol of emotions, regressive ego-level functioning, potential organicity) and dynamics (interpersonal attitudes, conflicts, emotional expression) can be reflected in the way a person copes with the visual-motor task set by the BVMGT. Her interpersonal withdrawal, constriction and conflicts around interdependent relationships are clearly mirrored in the manner in which she approached and carried out the task of interacting with a perceptual stimulus, imaging, conceptualizing and directing her fine motor coordination.

CASE: 03

AGE: 32

SEX: Female

Analysis of Copy Phase

A number of features catch our attention immediately. First, there are numerous small errors and distortions in the Gestalt which suggest a more pervasive and diffuse type of disorder in functioning. This woman does not accurately conceptualize, image and recreate reality; however, the type and degree of the distortions are relatively mild, suggesting that she probably has the capacity to do more accurate and careful reproductions.

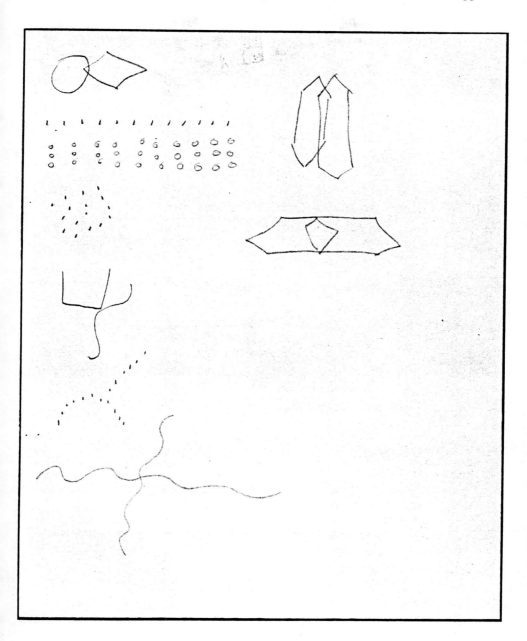

Case 03, Adult Copy

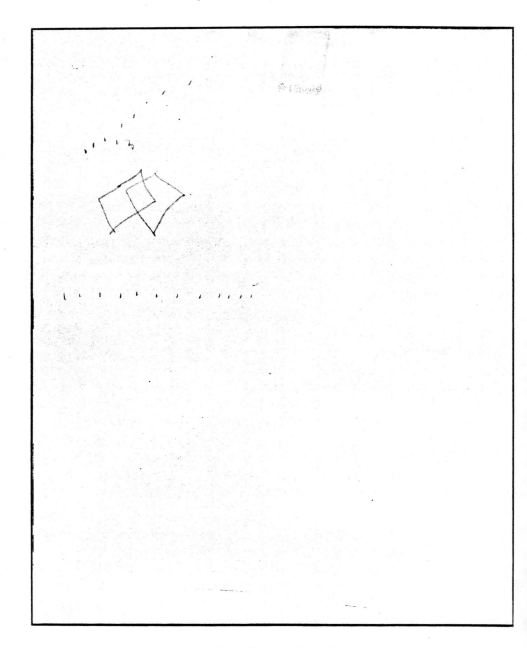

Case 03, Adult Recall

This type of diffusely distorted record, in our experience, is often found with persons who have a high intellectual capacity but feel under stress from intrapsychic and emotional conflicts at the time of the testing. This general inference appears clinically well supported since she was seeking voluntary hospitalization just prior to the administration of the Bender.

The second general feature which attracts our interest is related to the order of her productions. The figures began in the upper left corner and continued down the page, hugging the margin until space ran out. She then began at the top of the page, close to the other designs, and proceeded vertically again. This type of sequence tends to occur with persons who seek external structure in the environment to help them maintain the rigid and inflexible control they feel they need. They want to know what to expect and abhor change and surprises. Rigid, planned control is part of the way they also cope with their emotions and impulses, and as one might expect, such persons tend to have low self-confidence and low self-esteem.

This woman very likely uses a variety of intellectual defenses involving planning, repression and inhibitory control around feelings and conflicts. Often a predominant defense for such persons will be an obsessive-compulsive orientation. Many clinical features confirmed these inferences. She showed strong obsessive-compulsive defenses and rigidity with fear her controls were slipping (a primary reason she was seeking the structure of hospitalization).

Turning next to examine the individual designs, we see that Figure A is somewhat smaller than the stimulus design. Similarly, some shrinkage occurs in the other reproductions which suggests that she shrinks her life space somewhat although not to an extreme degree. The pervasive size distortion is further evidence of a general tendency to inhibit emotional reactivity. The square subpart of Figure A shows several slight errors — there is a lack of closure at one point, a slight crossover on the bottom point, and slight concaving of one straight line. Also, the joining penetrates the circle rather than being tangential to it. Taken together these distortions suggest subtle tendencies to be careless and at moments to act out her impulses and impatience. Symbolically, it further suggests that she distorts her relationships with males and sees male-female interactions as painful. This distortion of the Gestalt in Figure A may possibly indicate some sadomasochistic trends in her personality as well.

In Figure 1 she regressed slightly in functioning by turning the dots to small dashes which is often associated with angry feelings that slip past the person's controls. This expression of acted-out hostility is nevertheless contained and not allowed to proceed to a degree that the entire Gestalt of the figure is lost. The other designs having dots (Figs. 3 and 5) show a perseveration of this slight intradesign distortion, which suggests that in situations where she must concentrate, follow orders (copy the stimulus) and maintain control over distracting internal and external stimulation, she feels some frustration and anger which is expressed in subtle, possibly passive-aggressive ways. Her passive-aggressive tendencies are suggested by the fact that she did what she was told, but altered and distorted the product slightly.

Design 2 has numerous slight distortions also. She simplified the design, omitting one column of circles which is further evidence she is given to impatience and does not adequately follow through on tasks. The columns of circles show an angulation error, i.e. they are rotated clockwise in most instances with some unevenness at various points, although the overall orientation of Figure 2 is maintained. These errors are further evidence of a struggle with internal impulses which she handles by somewhat chaotic defenses. The clockwise rotation suggests an effort at inhibiting and dampening impulses while the unevenness both in angulation and in the quality of the circles suggests poor capacity for sustained controls. Here we would be interested in the F+% of the Rorschach and the quality of sustained control over articulation and discrimination of percepts to further clarify this component of her personality.

Design 3 has already been discussed in respect to changing the dots to dashes and shrinkage of size. The Gestalt of this design is also altered. She compressed the dots closely together, possibly reflecting both her tendency to withdraw and constrict her life space, especially around themes involving the open expression of aggression. Some tendency toward loss of control seen in the displacement of some of the dots from their appropriate position is also worthy of note since it further confirms the hypothesis that she has difficulty maintaining concentrated effort and sustained control.

Design 4 reveals an error of integration. The two subparts are slightly separated, and the apex of the sine wave is displaced downward, suggesting she has some discomfort around accepting her oral dependent needs. Cards A, 7 and 8, on the other hand, all reveal variations on the general hypothesis that she experiences more than average anxieties around interdependent relationships.

Often people who have schizoid tendencies involving inadequate separation and individuation, unclear sexual identification, and strong, anxiety-laden oral dependent needs will show this pervasive type of difficulty in making objects properly join. Information from the Thematic Apperception Test and the Rorschach would help clarify the nature of these interpersonal conceptions and identity problems. The possibility of mild or compensated central nervous system dysfunction is also a tenable hypothesis at this point.

Card 5 once again reveals numerous slight distortions which by this time have become sufficiently well supported to infer that she has pervasive difficulties in conceptualizing, imaging and maintaining control over fine motor coordination which are frequently encountered in persons with chronic intrapsychic conflicts and interpersonal anxieties that are partially compensated and controlled by a variety of defenses as well as average or better intelligence.

Hypotheses about the simplification of dots to dashes, omission of dots and internal variability of dot quality discussed in Cards 2 and 3 apply to Card 5 also. Symbolically, the widening of the opening at the base of the design is sometimes associated with oral themes and fears. Together with Design 4 this suggests she does have some oral dependency conflicts which interfere more than would ordinarily be expected for an adult.

Figure 6 once again shows her trend toward slight distortions of reality. The right horizontal sine wave is slightly flattened and elongated, suggesting a mild depressive tendency and/or a tendency to inhibit spontaneous emotional arousal. The way she reacted to color in the Rorschach should offer further insight into her manner of coping with emotional arousal. Slight distortions at the point of crossover joining also points to difficulties in her interpersonal relations which cause her some anxiety.

Figure 7 has many distortions. She shifted the leaning subpart to a vertical position parallel to the vertical subpart. The two figures were made almost identical, suggesting difficulties in individuation and separation. At times this type of error can signify homosexual trends and at other times is found associated with a lack of basic trust and an inability to give and receive support in interpersonal relationships. The other distortions, i.e. lack of closure, overrun and slight concaving in some straight lines, have already been discussed. Their appearance again in this figure only serves to reinforce prior hypotheses about the adequacy of her general functioning. Signs of conflict around sexuality in general and homosexuality in particular should be carefully explored in the other projective materials. Complaints of fear of loss of control are sometimes associated with homosexual panic which should not be overlooked as a possible source of stress in this person.

Numerous distortions appear in Figure 8, similar to previously-seen errors. Some lines are concave, some joinings are left open and/or overrun. The general impression is one of hastiness and carelessness of execution, which has been a repeated theme throughout her reproductions. On the whole this figure confirms prior inferences that her ego functions are diminished and that there are strong indications of chronic anxiety which limit her basic capacity to cope.

Analysis of Recall

The recall shows a startling degree of distortions and dimunition in reality level functioning. All figures are placed against the left margin which has the same implications as seen in the order of figures in the copy phase. Changes in Design 5 included a greater degree of simplification and downward angulation of the extended subpart. This change suggests that, when left on her own, her anxieties interfere with her reality level functioning and she feels impotent. Her judgment becomes impaired and her resources prove inadequate to sustain her in the completion of the task. Further evidence of the depletion of her resources is given in the small number of figures recalled. The WAIS would provide further information concerning her memory and reality level adaptation.

One figure is so grossly distorted as to be unrecognizable. It appears as two interpenetrating squares. The memory trace of images most likely to be the basis for this distorted figure could be any one of Figures A, 4, 7 or 8, although Figure 7 is the most likely. Such distortions usually occur only with severe ego deficiency, either of an organic or psychotic type. The Rorschach would give clarifying information about the extent and type of perceptual distortion and memory deficiency. This figure emphasizes previous hypotheses about her interpersonal and identity problems suggesting, moreover, that she has a tendency toward confused thinking and memory during those periods when she's left to judge things for herself.

Integration

This Bender record impresses one as being that of a person with chronic, moderate ego deficiencies who is experiencing intrapsychic stress.

The ego deficiencies are diffuse and pervasive, involving her ability to clearly image, conceptualize and sustain extended concentrated fine motor controls. She attempts to contain her anxiety and conflicts in a rigid, overcontrolled manner which quickly gives way and proves brittle under stress. Confusion and distortions creep into her memory trace, implying that her judgment becomes markedly impaired when left on her own.

The sources of the intrapsychic stress can only be hinted at in outline by the Bender. There are suggestions of diffuse interpersonal anxieties and conflicts involving her conception of human relationships as potentially painful. Sexual identity appears inadequately stabilized with hints that she may have homosexual inclinations. Problems around themes of oral dependency strivings, lack of basic trust and brittleness in adaptive capacity are implied as aspects of her personality functioning. The overall impression is that of a person with borderline psychotic adjustment with impending decompensation due to stresses either in her psychic life or in her real life. (These major hypotheses were well supported by other material in the test battery and clinical observations.)

Comment

This woman presented a not-infrequently-encountered type of Bender record for persons with ego deficiencies who are not now, and may never become, overtly psychotic. Their adjustment is rigid, causing them to regress or decompensate temporarily under internal or external stress. This inference was borne out in the Bender by the presence of the numerous, diffuse distortions without a deterioration of the Gestalt. Gross signs of ego deficiencies such as collisions, rotations or inability to execute angles were also not present. Except on the recall the deviations were sufficiently mild in most cases to indicate a good prognosis for recovery once the crisis in her life has been resolved or compensated. An ego-supportive type of therapy would be suggested for a person giving a Bender record of this type when the testing and clinical data supports these inferences.

CASE: 04

AGE: 48

SEX: Male

Analysis of Copy

Two features of this record are especially noteworthy. First, there is a high degree of disorganization in general with one collision (Figs. A and 6). This suggests that the general inference can be made that his personality is disorganized and he has a severe degree of impairment in his ability to conceptualize and maintain the boundaries between himself and others. Impairments of this degree in a person of his age are usually found when

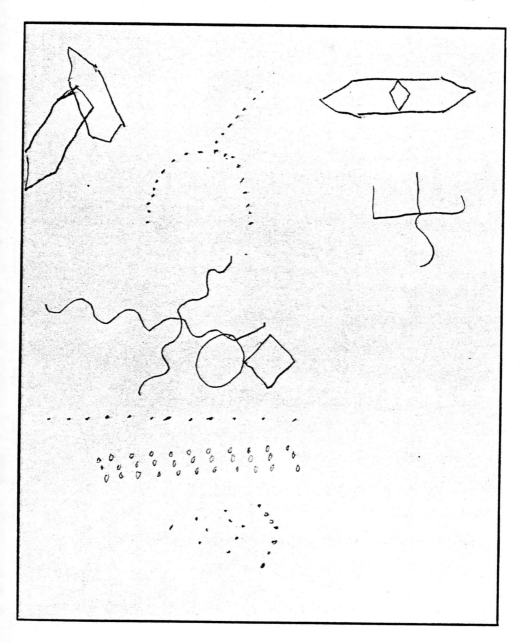

Case 04, Adult Copy

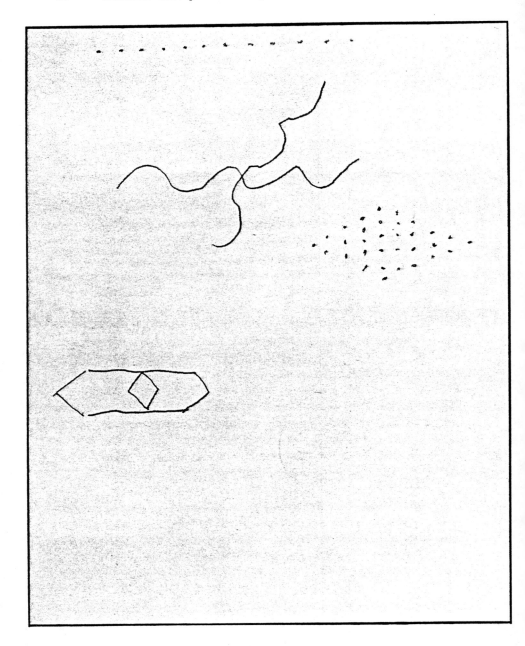

Case 04, Adult Recall

there is personality decompensation and/or organicity.

Second, the line quality reveals some shakiness, difficulty in maintaining a straight line, difficulty in making smooth sine waves and fairly heavy pressure. Any or all of these line quality features may be associated with emotional conflicts, concomitant anxiety and muscle tension or diffuse cortical dysfunction. Heavy line pressure may reflect emotional tension and at times a tendency to overreact emotionally — that is, to experience strong internal emotional reactions out of proportion to the realistic events. The overt reaction may be suppressed or acted out. If it is suppressed, he won't appear to others as an *emotional* person. In fact, we have observed some persons who are outwardly very inhibited but report the experience of very strong emotional reactions inwardly and who express surprise that other people do not recognize their emotional reactions. Inward tension and mood swings are also sometimes seen in the heavy line pressure of Bender reproductions. In this man's case the inference was fairly sound. He tended to appear quiet, calm and collected most of the time to others, but was experiencing intense internal turmoil.

Closer examination of the organization of the reproductions suggests refinements on the general inference that he is disorganized. He begins in the middle of the page, indicating a strong egocentric trend in his personality. He also begins somewhat low on the page which is often a sign of some depression. He then proceeds vertically down the page until he reaches the bottom. Up to this point he has proceeded methodically in an organized fashion. Thereafter he abruptly loses an orderly procedure and places designs primarily by choosing available spaces. This is similar to the type of organization seen in latency age children and indicates regression under stress.

The loss of an orderly procedure occurred when he was forced to change direction since he reached the bottom edge of the page. The abrupt loss of order suggests that he is rigid and inflexible in the organization of his life space. He sets out with a preconceived plan or approach, but when reality forces him to change directions he does not have the flexibility to adapt. Instead he gives up any attempt to reorganize his approach except at a very immature level. He can be expected to experience more than the usual degree of anxiety when he encounteres changes in his life and he probably has more than the average expected difficulty in changing the direction of his life.

Clinical data suggested that these inferences did have some behavioral manifestations. He was experiencing a very high degree of stress at the time of testing with the precipitating event being recent loss of work.

The next part of the analysis involves examination of each design for symbolic potential. Figure A reveals some line quality deficiency in the square subpart, suggesting that concepts of masculinity may cause anxiety. Slight distortions in the square subpart of Figure 4 as well as the angulation distortion of the sine wave on Figure 4 to resemble a phallic symbol are further hints that his conception of masculinity may cause him anxiety or be a matter of conflict. The exaggeration in size of Figure 5 is further evidence for the hypothesis that he is uncertain about his masculinity and at times tries to compensate for feelings of impotence by exaggerating masculine features, a phenomenon often referred to in psychodynamic theory as a *masculine protest*.

The joining difficulties seen in Design A and Design 4 indicate some tendencies toward fragmentation which are compensated. The point of joining in both Figures A and 4 is distorted and shows slight overwork. He showed greater effort in making the objects meet than in other parts of the designs which suggests that he feels interpersonal anxiety and works to compensate for a tendency to draw away from others. Symbolically there is a connotation that both male-female relationships and oral dependent relationships invoke some discomfort for him.

Figure 1 is fairly well composed with only a hint of distortion in some of the dots which suggests that he can function quite effectively some of the time. The slight distortions are so small that little interpretation can be given other than a mild tendency to regress and become expansive at times, but for the most part this is highly controlled. The evidence of some regression is further seen in both Designs 3 and 5 where the same phenomenon occurs. The overall Gestalt is maintained, but the stress of sustained effort leads sporadically to slight distortions of dots within the designs.

Figure 2 is also relatively well executed with minor unevenness and distortions among the individual circles. The whole figure has a minor (less than 45°) counterclockwise rotation. This feature, in addition to the subtle distortions seen in Figures 1, 3 and 5, and the concave curvature given to some straight lines in Figure 7 combine to suggest some acting-out potential. The top angles of the penetrating subpart of Design 7 are also truncated, a phenomenon sometimes associated with impatience in carrying out a difficult task. Individuals who *cutoff* parts of a complex design sometimes have a tendency to act impulsively when trying to resolve complex life situations. Suicide is sometimes a concomitant of this type of distortion. This man did in fact have a history of suicidal gestures.

Figures 4 and 5 have already been largely discussed. Figure 6 shows a sudden loss of clear and adequate reality boundaries in a collision with Figure A. Collisions are uncommon beyond the preschool level and therefore indicate a severe regression in this man's functioning. He does. not always plan ahead sufficiently. This condition can be caused by any number of factors including distractions due to anxiety and/or momentary preoccupation with internal conflicts. Whatever the basis, collision indicates severe ego impairment and reduced reality testing and judgment. The Rorschach would shed greater light on the extent of the regression as well as his capacity for recovery.

Other distortions also occurred on Figure 6. The line quality was poor, revealing a jerkiness and uneven flow which suggests an uneven modulation of emotion and impulse. In addition, other indications of shaky line quality together with the collision suggest the possibility of mild diffuse cortical dysfunction. The design is also rotated slightly clockwise, suggesting further evidence of depressive trends in his personality.

Figure 7 has been partially analyzed. The angulation is simplified, there is some workover, and lack of closure occurs at the joining of some angles. All of these are general indications of regression in efficiency of reality adaptation. The point of penetration was also displaced, further suggesting that relations between persons create anxiety for him. The leaning subpart of Figure 7 appears to be supporting and penetrating the usual vertical subpart which is reduced in size and rotated counterclockwise. One potential connotation of this distortion is that he feels he must support dependent others whom he feels should be supporting him. Moreover, he redefines and distorts this dependency relationship, more directly emphasizing the penetration suggesting a sadistic component in some of his close relationships.

Figure 8 shows the same type and degree of mild distortions of closure, runover and line quality seen in Figure 7 with similar implications adding weight to the general hypothesis of diffuse regression in efficiency of reality adaptation.

Analysis of Recall

The number of figures recalled was about average. All of the figures increased in size, suggesting that without external structure he becomes mildly expansive. Distortions occur in all the figures further suggesting as did the copy phase that he is inclined toward some regression in his functioning. Figure 6 is simplified, and the angulation of the sine waves continues to be irregular and of poor quality. There is a trend in his personality toward uneven emotional expression. Sometimes he is hasty and accentuates the aggressive components, and at other times he inhibits the smooth flow of emotion. This feature is sometimes seen in persons with conflicts concerning acknowledgment of their true inner feelings and the expression of hostile or aggressive impulses.

The Gestalt of Figure 3 is distorted in such a way that the aggressive thrust is distributed between two equal points which further suggests strong ambivalence about the direction of aggressive impulses. The suggestion of some controlled conflict and regression in the copy phase of Figure 3 is given new meaning in the recall. When he is in a structured situation with clear models for his self-expression he functions with some conflict and minor regressions from which he recovers. When he is left on his own, however, his judgment and memory can become quite distorted and are marked by ambivalence and indecision, especially in the area of self-assertion and expression of aggression. This distortion also implies the possibility that he could turn his aggression inward against himself. The clinical data about his suicidal attempts is relevant to these hypotheses.

Finally, Figure 8 reveals increased closure difficulties and overrun on some angles. These features suggest that he has some difficulty in adequately completing a task and may tend toward some carelessness and imprecision. The inner diamond does not completely join the outer trapezoid which, with cues from the copy phase, is further evidence of anxieties around object relations.

Integration

The general impression of this man is that of a person currently experiencing a high degree of internal conflict and stress with moments of fairly severe regression and diffuse impairments in ego level functions.

He appears to be a person who has a severe conflict concerning expression of aggressive impulses. At times this is seen as ambivalence, indecision and distortion of judgment. It is especially noted in situations where he must make independent decisions or where he must organize flexibly. He is rigid and his defenses are brittle, causing a breakdown in his personal planning and loss of boundaries when events force a change in his direction.

A more detailed understanding of his intrapsychic conflicts is less certain from the Bender alone. Other projective techniques, especially the TAT and Rorschach, could shed more light on the nature and degree of his regressions and capacity for recovery. Conflicts concerning dependency relationships are commonly found in persons showing the types and degrees of regression seen in this Bender record. The presence of collisions, disorganization and memory distortion are indications of ego level dysfunction more likely to be encountered in borderline psychotic and/or organic disorders than in neurotic disorders. Of course, a final differential diagnosis cannot be established from the Bender alone.

Comment

This record provides a picture of the ways in which diffuse ego dysfunctions may be manifested in the visual-motor productions of an adult. Hutt (1969) discusses at length the theoretical basis of inferences from Bender reproductions. We feel this record helps to emphasize that aspect of Hutt's discourse which is addressed to the Bender reproductions as a phenomenal experience involving conscious and subconscious elements. Clinical data largely supported the major inferences drawn about this man from his Bender reproductions. While such information does not constitute scientific validation, we feel it happens too often to be purely accidental and confirms the usefulness of the Bender as both an instrument for exploring visual-motor coordination and as a device for projective personality testing.

CASE: 05
AGE: 33
SEX: Male

Analysis of Copy

The degree of disorganization and relatively heavy line pressure is the first feature that catches our attention. The heavy line pressure indicates he uses considerable energy and may tend toward strong emotional reactions. This level of organization is more similar to a latency age child and strongly indicates he takes a rather chaotic approach to solving life's problems. There is a strong trend toward disorganization of his personality which when considered along with the many distortions evident in the record suggests he may be subject to confusion at times. The presenting clinical complaints make this first impression quite plausible. He was referred for testing for evaluation of memory deficiencies, confusion and a tendency toward becoming withdrawn.

The immediate diagnostic impression at the outset is that there is a relatively severe degree of regression in reality level adaptation resembling individuals who have either psychotic or organic conditions. The Rorschach and other projective devices would give further information about the quality of his judgment and reality testing. The disorganization would be expected to be seen in the

Case 05, Adult Copy

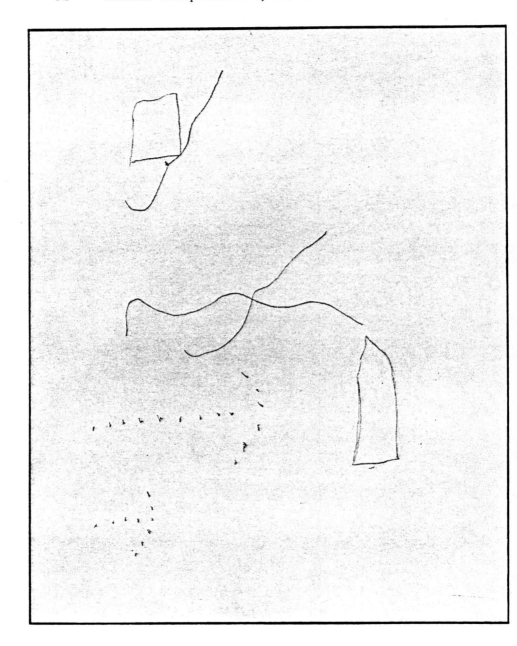

Case 05, Adult Recall

Rorschach in the quality of the analysis and synthesis of percepts. Memory deficiencies associated with organic impairment or psychotic intrusions are also sometimes revealed during the inquiry in the form of forgetting of percepts.

Turning briefly to the recall, there are clear signs of disorganization in the placement on the page. Memory loss and severe distortions with tendencies toward contamination are also evident and will be examined more closely in the analysis of the recall. For now it should be noted that there is much evidence of memory deficiencies which effect his imaging, conceptualizing and capacity for reproducing the designs which strongly indicates his complaints about memory loss are substantially based in observable cognitive deficiencies.

Returning to the analysis of the copy, note that Figure A is placed in the lower left quadrant, suggesting depression. It is rotated 180 degrees, suggesting that some form of perceptual-motor deficiency and/or personality characteristic is effecting his ability to image and accurately direct his actions.

Mild rotations are also evident in Figures 1, 2 and 7 which indicate a pervasive tendency toward spatial disorientation. Either personality conflicts and traits and/or diffuse cortical dysfunction can be associated with these types of errors.

Figure A has other mild distortions. The point of the square penetrates the circle slightly, suggesting there may be some sadomasochistic trends in his conception of male-female relationships. Some straight lines of the square are concaved slightly which is often indicative of impatience and a tendency to sometimes act out impulses, emotions or fantasies. Similarly, one line overruns the point of closure on the square which is further evidence of impatience and carelessness.

The circle is slightly larger than the square which, taken together with the other distortions of the square, may imply he has difficulties and anxieties around acceptance of masculinity. The full details of his view of himself and his sexual identity are not clear from the Bender. Distortions in the curved part of Figure 5 hint that there may be some moderate degree of *masculine protest* with a tendency to feel that women are dominant. The other projective devices would help more clearly define the nature of his sexual identity and conception of male-female relationships.

The Gestalt is maintained in Figure 1 with some minor errors. A very slight counterclockwise rotation suggests efforts at overcoming the depression noted in the placement of Figure A. Slight distortion of some of the dots and uneven spacing suggests the presence of factors that interfere with sustained fine motor coordination. Often anxiety, internal conflicts or low self-esteem with expectations of failure are found in persons treating Figure 1 in this manner. One dot is omitted, further strengthening the notion that he is careless and does not always adequately follow through on a task as was noted in the drawing of the square in Figure A.

Figure 2 is incomplete. He has omitted two columns of circles. In addition to the carelessness implied by this omission there is a possibility that he is withdrawn and preoccupied, which is consistent with the presenting complaints. He is very likely having fairly severe difficulty in taking his attention away from himself and his problems enough to pay careful attention to environmental demands. The digits span and arithmetic subscales of the WAIS would give further information about his concentration and attention. The picture completion subscale of the WAIS and the amount of D responses in the Rorschach would give further information about the degree he pays attention to details of the environment.

Figure 2 is also slightly rotated counterclockwise which gives more evidence of either an attempt to compensate for feelings of depression or a tendency to act out. The last three columns of circles almost collided with Figure 1. Some of the circles in the columns did collide with each other. Collision tendency indicates that he sometimes does not plan ahead adequately and may have to make last minute adjustments which impair the quality of his adaptation.

Figure 3 reflects a change in the order of the reproductions. The first three figures were placed vertically from top to bottom on the page. The order becomes chaotic after Figure 2, suggesting that his capacity for sustained concentration and planning is inadequate. He at first tries to bring order to his world but soon begins to regress to a lower level of functioning, placing figures haphazardly in open spaces in a manner similar to latency age children. (The amount and quality of W responses on the Rorschach would help define the nature of his capacity for planning and organization.)

Figure 3 is relatively well executed, showing he has a capacity for recovery from his regressions. Minor distortions reveal inner tensions which are controlled as is seen in the slight twisting scribble he makes for dots. He tends to blunt and constrict his aggressive impulses somewhat as is evidenced by the rounding of the angulations in Figure 3. This figure is the most difficult to organize which suggests he has some perceptual-motor capacities remaining to him that are approximately at an age-appropriate level.

Figure 4 has an error involving both a lack of joining and a displacement of the apex of the curved subpart upward in comparison to the point of contact it has with the open square. The separation suggests he has anxieties around his oral dependent needs.

The joining errors seen in Figures A, 7 and 8 are indications that he has tensions and anxieties around making contact with others. Sometimes he inappropriately fails to observe boundaries which suggests interpersonal conflict with some sadomasochistic orientation. At other times, especially around themes of giving or receiving nurturance, he also withdraws and avoids a direct contact.

The basic Gestalt of Figure 5 is retained with some slight modifications. Once again he simplified the figure slightly by omitting several dots from both subparts. The implications discussed for omissions on Figures 1 and 2 are further strengthened, showing a trend in his personality toward leaving tasks he undertakes uncompleted.

Figure 6 is close to the original Gestalt with some tendency toward decreasing the amplitude of the curves. This quality suggests he has a moderate degree of emotional flattening and lethargy sometimes seen in withdrawn and depressed states. Often the person who shows uneven flow in Figure 6 has difficulties expressing spontaneous emotion and lacks basic self-confidence in his ability to cope with the emotional impact of life. The degree of his impairment appears moderate, implying he still has some capacities for emotional expression and relatedness available to him.

The penetration error of Figure 7 has already been discussed. Symbolically this figure pulls for dependency connotations. Loss of angles and poor line quality suggest that anxiety with concomitant inattention may have been aroused by the symbolic pull of the figure. The leaning subpart of the figure is simplified by loss of angles and is overly absorbed, appearing to be supporting the upright figure. This configuration suggests he has more than the usual amount of difficulty around separation and individuation. Underlying feelings that he must support those on whom he depends for his own nurturant needs are very likely to be an aspect of his dynamics.

The blunt *cutting off* of the upper part of the leaning figure is sometimes encountered in persons inclined toward suicide. This suggestion of suicide, when viewed in the perspective of some depression in his record, is an alerting sign that should be taken into account when planning the course of treatment. There are implications also in Figure 7 because of the type and degree of the distortions that he has found close interdependent relationships engulfing and destructive. Loss of angles of the leaning figure suggests a view of relationships as castrating for the person who is dependent.

Several distortions appear in Figure 8. The most prominent is the misproportion of the right side of the figure and the disproportion of the center diamond. The rounding of the angles on the right side suggests uneasiness around themes of masculinity and emphasis on femininity. This latter hypothesis is given increased weight by mild distortions seen in Figures A and 5 previously discussed.

The center diamond is malformed, suggesting once more that dependency relationships are somehow destructive to the dependent person.

Analysis of Recall

The recall shows a startling increase in deterioration of Gestalt. Apparently, when he has to rely on his own resources, his judgment, reality testing and capacity for self-control markedly deteriorate.

All figures are simplified, indicating that the trends noted on the copy become more pronounced when he is in an unstructured situation. He has little patience and exercises poor self-control when left to himself. In a structured and guided situation he can perform much closer to the expectations for his age in respect to his abilities for effective reality testing and adaptation.

Taken as a whole the recall indicates a more severe underlying pathology than the copy indicated. The perseverated figure appears to be either a combination of Figures 1 and 3 or a distortion of Figure 3. If it is a combination of Figures 1 and 3, it is a contamination which suggests fluidity of perceptual and conceptual boundaries and is most apt to be found where there is a schizophrenic thought disorder. Evidence of contaminations (untenable blending of percepts and concepts) should be sought in the Rorschach. Confused thinking, bizarre ideation and the failure of repressive mechanisms allowing primary process thinking to emerge would also be expected to be evidence in the Rorschach. Furthermore, since he has better controls in a structures situation, he would be expected to perform well on the WAIS as compared to the Rorschach which is much more ambiguous.

Integration

This is the picture of a man who has pervasive, deep-seated conflicts around interpersonal relationships. The precise nature of these conflicts cannot be specified from a Bender analysis alone. There are hints and indications that he is currently very depressed and moderately withdrawn. He tends not to plan ahead adequately, is disorganized in his approach to life, and shows poor capacity for sustained concentrated effort. Reality testing is at times quite deficient, especially when he must rely on his own resources. When left on his own he deteriorates markedly, showing very poor judgment, expansiveness and a tendency toward thought disorder.

In many ways this man resembles persons who have chronic low self-esteem and insufficient self-confidence to achieve on their own. There are suggestions in the record that he has developed a view of himself as inadequate with expectations that his nurturant needs will not be met. He appears to expect that close interpersonal, interdependent relationships lead to pain and destruction.

The general diagnostic impression is that of a borderline psychotic person who is currently experiencing stress from either intrapsychic conflicts or environmental events. He has relatively few resources for coping effectively on his own but does have sufficient resources to respond to external guidance and structure.

If the patterns seen in the Bender are confirmed by other tests and general information, the final diagnosis would most probably be some type of functional disorder. Central nervous system dysfunction can never be ruled out by the Bender (See Hutt, 1969, Chap. 3). However, in the present instance the picture is more similar to functional impairment due to moderate to severe anxiety, depression and personality conflicts which are distorting his reality level functioning. The fact that he could at times maintain proper integration, angulation and line quality suggests that intrapsychic factors and conflicts are more likely to be the underlying basis for the distortions than organicity. A full test battery and neurological examination should be performed before reaching a final diagnosis and treatment plan.

Comment

This record illustrates how the Bender Gestalt can provide leads to understanding the degree of impairment and the nature of the disorder as seen in a depressed and withdrawn adult. Like Case 02, adult, the final diagnostic impression was that of a borderline psychotic personality. By contrast to Case 02 the specific features of the way this man copes, where he succeeds and how he fails are quite different. For example, whereas the woman (Case 02) was highly constricted, this man (Case 05) tended toward expansiveness.

Yet, a careful study of Case 02 and Case 05 illustrates how the Bender can frequently reveal not only an individual's unique characteristics, but also provide information which will help the clinician to formulate which general diagnostic category an individual may share in common with others. Case 02 and Case 05, for example, can *both* be considered borderline psychotic because their degree of regression and poor reality level adaptation is marked but not as manifest as in a case of overt, acute psychosis (see Case 10, adult). Hutt (1969) presents other Bender protocols involving a variety of diagnostic categories as well as studies and rationale related to configurational analysis. The reader is directed to these sections of Hutt's work for a more extensive discussion of the problems of differential diagnosis from the Bender Gestalt.

CASE: 06
AGE: 35
SEX: Male

Analysis of Copy

The spacing on the page is the most outstanding feature of this man's reproductions which command our attention first. He clustered the reproductions so tightly toward the top of the page that he was able to fit two thirds of the drawings into about one third of the available space. He began Figure A in the top left hand corner and then proceeded to tightly group together the remaining designs.

Compression of drawings into a small area of the page is usually representative of the performance of a person who has a tendency to withdraw from the environment. The world is ordinarily viewed as hostile and threatening by such persons. They tend to feel a strong need to cling to some place or someone to gain security. The dynamics of such a personality often includes denied hostile and aggressive impulses which are projected onto others. From clinical experience such persons have also been frequently found to maintain hostile dependent relationships with others. Whether any or all of these correlates of this type of Bender performance are true of this person would have to be determined from other features of his protocol and other information about him. The presenting clinical problem was at least consistent with these formulations. He had recently taken an

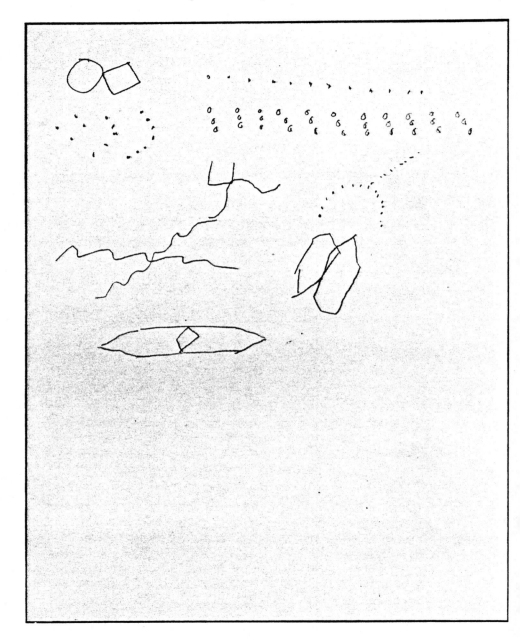

Case 06, Adult Copy

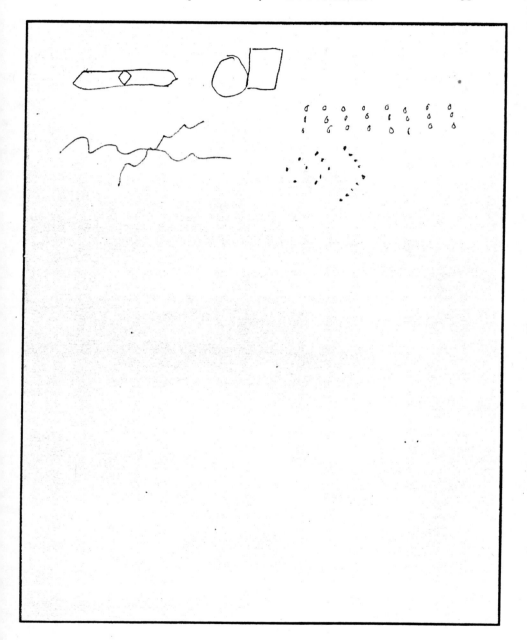

Case 06, Adult Recall

overdose of drugs and was anxious and depressed.

Overall, the Gestalt of the figures is sufficiently preserved to suggest that his basic capacities for reality testing and judgment are fairly well intact. Numerous minor errors suggest that either intrapsychic conflicts, mild organicity and/or moderate, diffuse regression under external stress is present. The sequence of the reproductions began with a left-right order, shifted to a vertical order, then returned to a left-right sequence again. One change of direction tends to be associated with some flexibility in problem solving. Two changes begin to reflect a mild degree of personality disorganization and suggest he may have some tendency to approach planning and arranging his life in a somewhat disorganized fashion after an initial orderly beginning.

The individual designs should shed some light on more specific components of his personality beyond the general trends noted above. He reduced the size of Design A, a feature true to a moderate degree of all the designs. This characteristic is further evidence that he feels vulnerable and shrinks back or withdraws from a world he expects will be hostile or threatening to him. Lack of basic trust in oneself and in others is often involved in this style of coping and defense. He very likely does not feel he can easily or readily meet the demands of life for competition or self-assertion.

A second feature of Design A is the slight downward rotation which is often associated with either flattening of affect or depression. Figures 1, 4, 5, 6 and 7 similarly show mild clockwise rotations suggesting a pervasive mild tendency to flatten or inhibit emotional expression with a potential for depression. It is noteworthy that the degree of these personality trends is mild which suggests that events in his current life situation may be precipitating factors for his reported depression more than chronic severe personality conflicts. The other projective tests would help delineate the presence and degree of these trends in his personality. Many features of the Rorschach can reflect depression and indicate his style of experiencing and coping with emotions.

Figure 1 shows mild distortion in that one dot is converted to a circle (a simplification) and the other dots are turned into small squiggles reflecting highly-contained tension associated with concentrated, goal-directed activity. Often such squiggle marks reveal a personality trend toward anger and hostility when faced with the necessity for frustration tolerance and concentration. He kept the squiggle marks small and the horizontal plane even, suggesting that if he felt anger he largely inhibited the impulse and it did not grossly disrupt his reality level adaptation.

The downward slant suggests a mild depressive trend which in view of the inhibited hostility could indicate a tendency to internalize anger and turn aggression toward himself.

Figure 3 gives further indication that he blunts aggressive impulses. The clinical data concerning a suicide attempt and depression lend credibility to the impression given by the analysis of the record, thus far that one component of his personality is a tendency to inhibit aggressive and hostile impulses with resultant depressive mood swings.

Figure 2 is grossly within expectancy, although there is a mild distortion of Gestalt. The design was reproduced as more elongated than in the stimulus card. There is also minor unevenness in the size of the circles and fluctuations of angle in the columns. The columns are also moderately uneven in the horizontal plane. Together these minor deviations suggest the presence of internal tensions and momentary mood swings. He experiences more than the usual degree of difficulty in sustaining the concentrated, goal-directed effort involved in imaging, conceptualizing and directing his visual-motor coordination. This man very likely wants to relate to people but experiences considerable internal tension and conflict with denial and repression being likely defense mechanisms.

Figure 4 shows a rotation of the curved subpart with shakiness in line quality. Since the circle of Figure A was grossly within expectancy, the difficulties seen in this figure suggest that oral dependent themes may cause him tension and anxiety. The clockwise rotation suggests that he may be pessimistic and fearful about meeting his oral dependent needs. Information from his history would probably show poor object relations and insecurity around nurturant mother figures. The clinical presentations of depression would, of course, be consistent with this hypothesis of unmet oral needs.

Figure 5 reveals further indications of a depressive tone in the slight clockwise rotation and shows the tensions noted earlier in the very slight slashing of the dots and disorganization of spacing. The evidence is accruing that he is a person who struggles with internal conflicts, especially involving the denial and repression of hostile impulses. His reaction to Design 5 further suggests he may have a tendency to feel impotent in the sense of being unable to express masculine assertiveness. He is very likely dissatisfied with the constriction in his personality and the implied inability to be forthright and discharge tension openly.

Figure 6 is mildly distorted. Most of the curves are made more angular, suggesting emphasis on masculine symbolism and a tendency for hostile affect to be predominant. This man would be expected to be somewhat flat in his affect but at times would show hostility. The potential for diffuse, partially-compensated organicity must also be considered. Often organically-impaired persons will have difficulty changing directions and will show poor line quality and lack of smoothness. Figures 4, 7 and 8 all show some evidence of shaky line quality which could be either a product of mild organicity or internal conflicts and tensions.

Figure 7 is poorly connected with overruns, lack of closure and poor line quality, suggesting inadequate attention and concentration and a rather careless attitude toward the task. Often such productions imply fearfulness of people based on early dissatisfying relationships. Lack of closure at the bottom of the leaning figure suggests he may at times have poor control over his drives and impulses which can leak through his efforts at blunting and repression. He may be overtly hostile at times.

Penetration of the leaning figure is decreased, and the two figures become almost parallel, suggesting a lack of adequate autonomy and differentiation between himself and others. The entire figure is rotated counterclockwise, reinforcing the earlier hypothesis of a depressive tone. Moreover, the Gestalt of the reproduction suggests imagery of one figure pushing over another, possibly implying that he feels his dependency needs are not adequately supported by persons on whom he relies or that he feels his needs are overwhelming.

Figure 8 shows numerous minor errors. Some angles are disconnected, one angle shows overrun, and the center diamond is misshapen and poorly connected at the bottom. Line quality is mildly shaky. The previous hypotheses about inner tensions and some carelessness in an otherwise compulsive orientation receive further support. He has a moderate degree of difficulty in joining objects together and tolerating the frustration of sustained goal-directed activity.

Analysis of Recall

An average number of figures were recalled, suggesting an average level of intellectual functioning. The tendency toward constriction in the size of the figures and in the spacing between figures is even more pronounced than in the copy. When left on his own he becomes more fearful of asserting himself, clings more closely to structures and supports and exerts a tighter control over his emotions and reactions. Such a withdrawal indicates strong feelings of inadequacy, lack of self-confidence and projection of fearful qualities onto others.

Figure A is distorted at the point of joining which is displaced downward and in the elongation of the square turning it into a rectangle. The exaggeration of the square suggests conflicts around his masculinity, especially as it relates to male-female interactions. The increased size suggests feelings of inadequacy and a compensatory desire to dominate the sexual relationship. The displacement of the point of junction is similar to the displacement seen in Figure 7 of the copy and strengthens the hypothesis that close relationships cause anxiety for him. He wants to maintain a relationship which does not involve direct assertiveness and open communication. He would like to be dominant in heterosexual relationships but lacks the self-confidence and ability to assert himself directly. At times, however, he may put on a bluff of dominance.

Figure 8 is somewhat better composed than in the copy, suggesting that anxiety and tension may very likely have contributed to the distortions in the copy. To some degree he is better able to integrate when left on his own. This improvement does not last, however, as the remaining designs show numerous flaws, suggesting his performance is variable which may make him somewhat puzzling to others. He is unpredictable. At moments he can function quite well, yet he is unable to sustain the higher level functioning and soon shows regressions.

Figure 2 is simplified, omitting three columns of circles, suggesting he does not carry through well when he must rely on himself. Unevenness in spacing, angulation of columns and lateral plane all confirm the earlier impression from the copy of chronic internal tensions with partially successful efforts at control.

Figure 6 by comparison with the copy has changed relatively little. Poor impulse modulation with variations between increasing and decreasing affect is evident. Hostility is suggested in the increased sharpness of angulation and attempts at controlling and flattening emotional arousal are seen in the decrease in amplitude of the sine waves. His defensive maneuvers around control of aggressive impulses are mildly chaotic. The increased angulation in the vertical plane could imply his aggression is directed toward authority figures.

Figure 3 is close to the copy but somewhat more constricted, and angulation is slightly increased. An increase in angulation was also seen in Figures A and 6, pointing to the likelihood that when he is in an ambiguous situation his aggression becomes more evident. The constriction seen in this record could very well be either an action defense or a reaction formation against aggressive and hostile feelings.

Integration

This is the picture of a person who has a view of the world as hostile and threatening. He does not have very much trust in himself or in others with whom he forms relationships. His major defensive maneuver is to constrict and withdraw in the face of expected harm and threat from others.

Many features of his personality reflect chronic internal tensions and conflicts which he attempts to control by denial, repression and flattening of affect. A primary theme emerging from his manner of interacting with the Bender Gestalt was his fear of his own assertiveness and aggression which is partially controlled by avoiding close interaction with others. He seeks a relationship with others marked by avoidance of direct confrontation or dominant assertiveness. In many ways he resembles persons who have not experienced healthy and satisfying early relationships in which the expression and appropriate modulation of impulses was tolerated. There is a high likelihood of chronic anger around unmet dependency needs and pessimism over being able to get his needs met.

The depressive tone seen throughout his productions could reflect either a chronic pessimistic outlook on life, a reaction to his current personality conflicts, or a reaction to loss of some important object or relationship. From the Bender Gestalt alone it is not clear if one or all of these factors underly the depression.

The overall impression is that of a man who has long-standing intrapsychic conflicts with anxiety, flattening of affect and a tendency toward depression and withdrawal. Much more information would be needed to confirm or reject these inferences.

Comment

This Bender protocol was instructive in that it showed relatively mild degrees of distortion, many of which might not be scoreable by one or another of the scoring systems (Hutt, 1969; Koppitz, 1972), yet it revealed many rich themes and pointed to hypotheses concerning how this man functions considering some of the major personality characteristics and dynamics he possesses. Clinical information later amply supported the major inference of a withdrawn person who has anxiety and conflicts that interfere with his close personal relationships.

CASE: 07
AGE: 24
SEX: Male

Analysis of Copy

One outstanding characteristic of this record is the difficulty

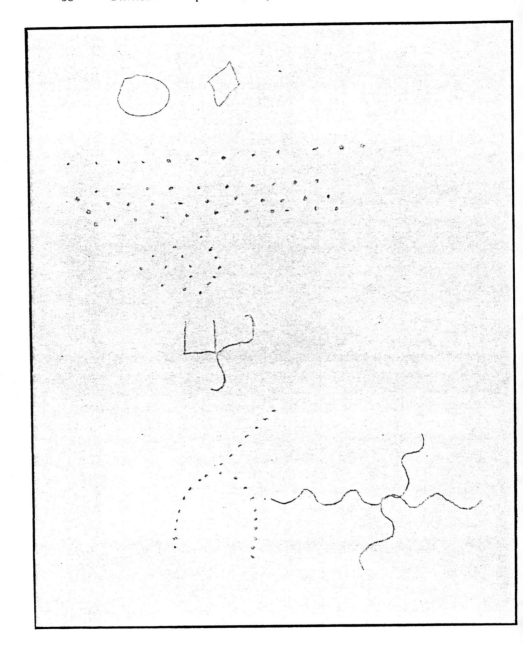

Case 07, Adult Copy

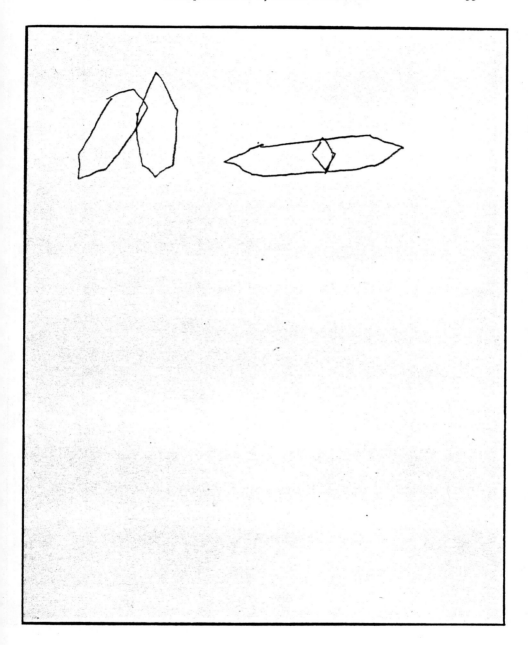

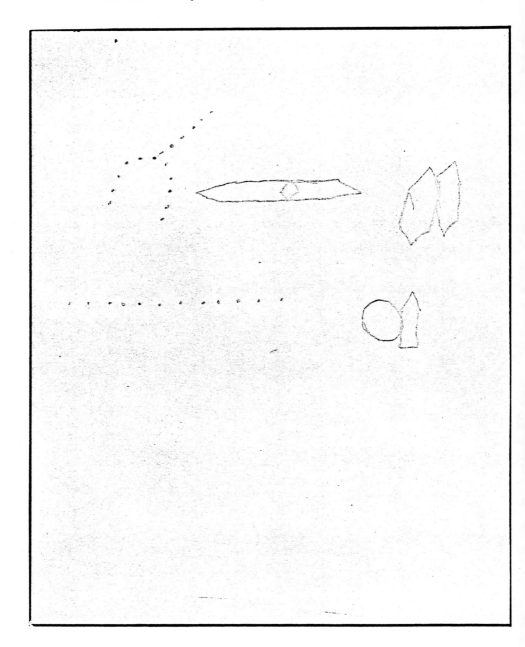

Case 07, Adult Recall

seen in the joining of the compound figures. Figures A, 4, 6, 7 and 8 in varying degrees indicate that this man is very concerned about bringing objects together and connecting subparts of designs. Anxiety concerning interpersonal relations is frequently a personality component of individuals who show this type of Gestalt distortion. Often they are persons who have not enjoyed rewarding or dependable relationships during their early years. This leaves them with a tendency to expect hurt or disappointment from others.

The integration distortion could, of course, also be associated with diffuse cerebral dysfunction. This inference receives some support from the shaky line quality and distortions of the circular forms. Information from the Wechsler Performance Subscales and the Rorschach would be helpful in making a final distinction concerning extent and nature of organicity versus psychopathology. What is clear at this point is that there is a moderate to severe degree of ego impairment evident regardless of whether it is based on organicity or intrapsychic and personality factors. Further evidence of ego impairment comes from a moderate degree of expansiveness reflected by his reproduction of Figures 7 and 8 on a separate sheet of paper. This was done despite the fact that there was sufficient space left on the one sheet he had been instructed to use.

We expect that the analysis of individual designs may shed more light on these general first impressions. Clinical information at least tentatively corroborated the impression of ego impairments. Presenting complaints included drug abuse, sociopathic behavior, somatization and blackouts.

Figure A shows a wide separation with distortions in both subparts, suggesting conflicts and anxiety concerning interpersonal relations. The symbolism of this figure suggests more specifically that he has anxieties and withdrawal/avoidance tendencies concerning male-female relationships. Some shakiness in line quality reflecting poor coordination could also imply the presence of anxiety. The square figure is reduced in size and more poorly reproduced than the circle. This suggests the possibility that he feels males are somehow inferior to females and are inadequate or flawed in some way. The suggestion of inadequacy feelings is strong both from the symbolic theme and the quality of the Gestalt of the reproductions. Sexual identity formation should be explored through clinical interviews and examination of other projective techniques.

Figure 1 essentially maintains the Gestalt with some tendency toward expansiveness. Individual dots begin precisely and gradually enlarge, suggesting he at first constricts and contains his impulses but under the pressure of concentrated goal-directed attention begins to experience more internal turmoil and difficulty in containing his impulses. The overall mild tendency toward expansiveness discussed earlier is specifically suggested by this figure. Anxiety accompanying feelings of inadequacy and impotence with relatively low frustration tolerance are often associated with tendencies toward expansiveness.

The fact that Figures A, 1, 3, 4 and 6 are constricted while Figures 1, 5 and 7 are mildly enlarged suggests that he experiences mood swings related to ambivalence. Since there is distortion of visual-motor functioning, most likely his ambivalence is fairly strong and his mood swings are much wider than average.

Figure 2 is fairly well reproduced in terms of the overall maintenance of Gestalt and horizontal plane. Some distortion is seen in converting circles to dots. There is no way to be certain whether this reflects perseveration from Design 1 or a retrogression. Using Hutt's scoring for retrogression (1969) we see evidence that he has a relatively severe and chronic defensive pattern. This suggests some degree of failure in integration and ego-level functioning. The evidence of deficiencies in integration noted earlier plus the contamination of Figure A with 7 in the recall further suggest ego deficiencies of a type and degree which tend to occur in schizophrenia.

Figure 3 is compact and about one-fourth smaller than the stimulus design in the lateral plane. The vertical plane is about the same as the stimulus. This reduction in size suggests some constriction and withdrawal tendencies. It is interesting to note the variation in withdrawal and expansive tendencies. Figure A was decreased in size. Figure 1 was somewhat expansive, but Figure 2 mildly tended toward constriction, a trend which continued and increased until Figure 5, which was again expansive.

Figure 6 then was constricted and Figure 7 was mildly expansive with Figure 8 being about accurate. Overall these fluctuations in size suggest internal conflict and anxieties which he handles in an ambivalent fashion. At one time he begins to act out his impulses, reaching into the environment and at other times he constricts, pulling back into himself and away from people.

Figure 4 is quite constricted in size and the curved subpart has shaky line quality and distortion of angulation. Angulation errors in curved parts generally reflect difficulty in dealing with affect and control of impulses. This may be related to organicity, impulse modulation difficulties and/or mental retardation. Clinical information as well as the recall of five figures made mental retardation highly unlikely. Such difficulties have been found to differentiate well-adjusted from poorly-adjusted persons which strengthens previous impressions that this man's object relations are poor. The clinical information that he was acting in a sociopathic fashion is consistent with the hypothesis of poor adjustment and impulse modulation difficulties.

The symbolism of Figure 4 suggests that he has unresolved conflicts and anxieties concerning nurturant needs. The presenting complaint of drug abuse is consistent with this inference. In many instances persons with drug abuse problems have severe emotional deprivation extending back into the very early years of their development. The evidence is quite strong that he has ego impairments which very likely involve at least in part early developmental deficiencies in nurturant relationships. These have left him insecure and lacking in self-confidence. He would be expected to have difficulties in close relationships, especially in areas which involve giving or receiving help and support.

Figure 5 shows marked expansion and suggests masculine symbolism has special significance for him. The curved part is exaggerated, suggesting strong oral dependent needs. The slight clockwise rotation of the figure suggests some disequilibrium is present. Displacement of the extension is further indication of integration difficulties in general and in this figure suggests anxiety about his sexual identity. Altogether Figure 5 indicates the presence of some anxiety concerning masculine identification and sexuality. The exaggerated size may very well be overcompensation or *masculine protest* for underlying feelings of inadequacy.

Figure 6 reflects curvature distortions and size reduction, both of which have been observed in other figures and commented on previously. This figure reinforces the previous inferences that he experiences difficulties with affect and interpersonal relatedness and/or has a moderate degree of diffuse brain dysfunction.

Figures 7 and 8, as previously noted, were placed on a separate sheet of paper, suggesting an expansive trend in his personality which is often associated with rebelliousness and unwillingness to accept reality boundaries. Acting out of impulses and fantasies sometimes accompanies such expansiveness. The information that he was referred partially for sociopathic behavior is consistent with the notion that he at times ignores the terms set by society and acts with poor judgment.

Figure 7 reveals numerous subtle distortions. Line quality is poor, especially at the base of the design where some straight lines are made concave. This feature suggests anxiety and a tendency for his controls to be weak under the impact of drive arousal. The point of intersection is reduced, suggesting the before-mentioned tendency to withdraw somewhat from close interpersonal relations. This implies that dependency relationships have been uncomfortable for him.

Figure 8 is rotated slightly counterclockwise, suggesting a mild tendency to act out at times. As in Figure 7 the line quality is shaky and there are some tendencies toward making straight lines concave. As in Figure 7 one angle has a very slight closure error. These errors imply anxiety and some carelessness. The inference of anxiety is further strengthened by the sketching of the center diamond, implying that dependency relationships are a source of anxiety for him, reinforcing this same inference from Figure 4 and Figure 7.

Analysis of Recall

Five figures were recalled, implying an average level of memory functioning. The figures are largely contained in the upper half of the page. This suggests that when he is left to his own resources he constricts somewhat as compared to when he is in a more structured situation. The hypothesis from the copy that he is a person who lacks self-confidence to a significant degree is strengthened by his treatment of space in the recall.

Figure 5 is simplified by a reduction in the number of dots and is rotated clockwise. The Gestalt was preserved and the expansiveness seen on the copy was reduced. He seems to have largely recovered from his earlier reaction to Design 5, flattened his affect and achieved a better integration on the recall. This phenomena in our experience can be related to many psychodynamic features which affect regression and recovery in a person. A likely hypothesis here is that he suppressed and-or repressed the earlier anxiety-provoking associations and simplified the task, thereby gaining an improvement in integration.

The tendency to simplify is evident also in Design 8 where there is a loss of angles, in Design 7 where he reduced the penetration of the design and omitted an angle, and in Design A which is contaminated (the square replaced by a simplified Design 7 subpart). This is a severe degree of simplification which implies a reduction of cathexis to the task. He tends not to invest himself in tasks when he is left on his own. There is some tendency toward carelessness.

Figure 1 is well reproduced, suggesting as in Figure 5 some constriction has taken place as compared to the copy. One possible inference for the phenomenon of improvement of a design on recall is hostility toward authorities. The examiner and the instructions to copy the stimulus card arouse angry feelings for some persons who have chronic hostility toward authorities. These feelings which may be suppressed then act to increase tension and lead to the mild distortions seen in the copy of Figure 1. On recall the person may feel less under direct command, bringing about a lessening of the tension and improvement in the product.

Figure 7 is decreased in size and has poor line quality and joining errors. The dependent figure is larger than the supporting figure, suggesting a blurring of child-adult roles with the child giving more support than the adult. Such role reversals are often found in persons who have severe underlying emotional deprivation which is consistent with the impression gathered in the copy of strong underlying oral dependent needs. The figures placed in parallel are sometimes seen with homosexuality. Since the parallel figures occurred on recall there is a suggestion that there may be latent homosexual trends which he keeps covered in conventional structured situations. Information from the other projective devices such as drawings, TAT and Rorschach and from clinical interviews would shed further light on his psychosexual adjustment.

Figure A is contaminated which is usually a sign of formal thought disorder similar to contaminations on the Rorschach. Perceptual cognitive functioning, level of reality judgment and capacity for perceptual integration should be investigated in the Rorschach. Symbolically this contamination suggests his conception of male-female interactions may have some bizarre qualities.

Integration

This is the picture of a person who has marked disturbances in his capacity for integration. Object relations reflect strong underlying oral dependent strivings which are suppressed and denied. He expects that close interpersonal relations will lead to anxiety and suffering which he tries to avoid by withdrawing to a moderate degree. The capacity for relatively intact reality testing and some relatedness to others remains when he is not overly anxious. There are suggestions that sexual identity is not clearly or firmly defined with some indications that his judgment may be most distorted and his avoidance tendencies most acute in this area.

Numerous soft signs of diffuse cerebral dysfunction which were consistent with the presenting complaint of blackouts penetrate this man's performance. Signs of organicity should be carefully evaluated in the Wechsler Adult Intelligence Scale and the Rorschach to compliment and complete the picture. The combination of integration deficiencies, expansiveness with ambivalence and a contamination on the recall strongly suggest ego impairments similar to those found in borderline psychotic conditions or mild schizophrenic conditions. Drug abuse can induce a variety of symptoms resembling either psychotic or organic conditions. No final differential diagnosis can be made from the Bender alone.

Comment

This record presented a person who was clearly not functioning at an age-appropriate level, yet was also not sufficiently disturbed to be considered in an acute state. Comparison of this record with Case 08 or Case 10 is instructive in terms of the much greater degree of ego integration seen in this man's performance than in those of the latter cases.

The difficulties inherent in differential diagnosis are also instructive in the present case. While there can be no question that the Bender reproductions reflect regressed and inefficient reality adaptation, there are numerous conditions that can lead to such regression, ranging from intense anxiety and intrapsychic conflict to psychosis and organicity.

The Bender analysis provides many leads and gives much information about level of reality functioning, adaptation and potential organicity. When taken together with information from other sources in the test battery and other clinical information it is helpful in coming to understand the whole person and his unique patterns of strength and weakness. We find this type of understanding to be most helpful in planning the management of the treatment process.

CASE: 08

AGE: 42

SEX: Female

Analysis of Copy

Gross regression and distortions of Gestalt are evident in this woman's reproductions, suggesting severe ego impairments. Wide variations in the sizes of the figures and pressure of the pencil suggest strong internal tensions and ambivalence often found in persons who feel confused and whose reality testing is

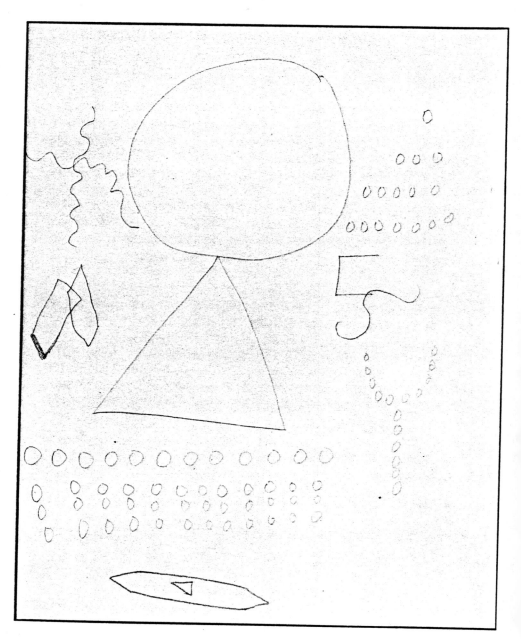

Case 08, Adult Copy

Case 08, Adult Recall

impaired. The expansive use of space suggests pressures exist for personality decompensation.

The distortion of the square subpart of Figure A and the diamond in Figure 8 into triangles further indicates a state of severe regression in functioning with a strong possibility of a formal thought disorder. The presenting problems were consistent with these general inferences. She was highly anxious and depressed and exhibited paranoid ideation with auditory hallucinations and a history of recent alcoholism.

The sequence of the figures is rigid. She began in the center of the page, suggesting strong egocentrism and proceeded vertically. Thereafter she maintained a vertical order. Her judgment was poor in that she did not use very much forethought or planning to allow enough space for all the designs. She still had some capacity for planning remaining intact; she was able to adjust the size of the designs to fit the available space without collisions. Although her personality organization is rigid and brittle, she still has the ability to plan and integrate to some degree.

Quality of perceiving, cognition and judgment should also be evaluated from the other tests in the battery. The Wechsler Adult Intelligence Scale would provide information about quality of reality level thinking and adaptation under structured conditions. The other projective devices can give further information about reality testing, cognition, perception and dynamics.

Perseveration, in terms of converting dots to circles, is seen in Figures 1, 3 and 5 and in the curved parts of Figure 6. Figure 2 has one column of circles too many and Figure 5 is simplified to include fewer units than the stimulus. Overall these errors suggest a highly erratic quality to her reality testing and ability to carry out goal-directed tasks with stability, evenness and perseverance. In general her performance suggests a marked decrease in spontaneity and ego controls. Analysis of color responses in the Rorschach would aid in gaining an understanding of how she copes with her emotions.

Numerous rotations are evident. Figures A, 3, 4 and 5 are rotated 90 degrees. This factor is most often found in records of persons who are psychotic, mentally defective and/or organic. This degree and type of error is further evidence of a profound disturbance in ego functions.

Oppositional tendencies and passive aggressive traits are frequently observed in clinical work with psychotics and suggest that the other test indicators and general information on this woman would help clarify this inference. Rotations in a clockwise direction are often associated with depression as well, and this is consistent with the presenting complaint of depression in this woman.

The individual designs can help suggest leads to strengths and weaknesses beyond the generalizations made from the errors that occur across numerous designs.

Figure A is grossly enlarged, occupying a significant portion of available space. This suggests she is a person who placed herself in the center of attention and very likely has difficulty acknowledging other people's needs or being objective in her judgment. There is a strong possibility of autistic logic which should be checked against her performance on the Rorschach.

The circle is placed in a dominant position and the square is distorted into a triangle, suggesting she views women as dominant over men. The exaggerated size also suggests an overcompensation for feelings of inadequacy — that is, an effort to appear *larger* and stronger when she feels small and weak. The clinical picture of a very dependent woman and paranoid ideation reinforce this latter inference.

Figure 1 is approximately correct in lateral size and is set against the margin, suggesting she compensated for the initial expansiveness and became somewhat more realistic. She also retreated to the margin, suggesting Figure A may have been an unrealistic bluff of power which she could not maintain and which she quickly abandoned for a safer, more structured position. Strong dependency needs are suggested which enter into and determine her behavior to a significant degree. The regression seen in converting dots to circles in Figures 1, 3 and 5 is further evidence of dependency and immaturity as major components of her personality.

The dependency theme is very strong. Figure 4 has numerous errors as do Figures 7 and 8, all giving additional weight to the inference she has chronic anxiety and conflict around dependency. Figure 4 was drawn like a receptical or *box* on its side, suggesting she feels empty. Persons with strong oral deprivation will sometimes draw Design 4 in this fashion, symbolizing their feelings of chronically unmet needs for nurturance. The exaggeration of the curved aspect and the displaced point of joining are indicative of anxieties around oral gratifications. The clockwise rotation suggests pessimism and depression about getting her needs met.

Returning to Figure 2 we find again her need to cling to the margin. The Gestalt is grossly preserved with some mild clockwise rotation in the columns and a mild error of perseveration, i.e. one additional column of circles. She begins the figure more expansively, showing the overall trend toward expansion at the beginning of a task which later gives way to constriction. The earlier interpretations about this tendency would apply here also.

In Figure 3 we observe a major rotation and errors in Gestalt. The dots are converted to circles and the angulation is flattened. She tends to flatten, suppress or repress her aggression. The tendency toward depression noted previously is elaborated by this figure. Under the impact of unacceptable angry feelings and impulses she tends to regress to a more immature level of functioning. The anger is directed toward herself, in part, resulting in depression and in part she has very likely denied the anger and projected it onto others. The reported paranoid ideation and auditory hallucinations make this formulation of her dynamics quite probable.

Figure 4 has already been discussed with need for only one further comment in the light of Figure 3. The strong unmet dependency needs inferred for Figure 4 could be the basis of chronic rage and pessimism which are not infrequently aspects of depression. Especially in psychotic depression, anger against an introjected object can be one aspect of the oral fixation. Of course, there are other aspects to depression, and this dynamic may or may not fit this person. Depression is often a reaction to loss of loved objects. This feature of her record would make us want to explore her history to see if there were any deaths, separations or divorces in the recent past which may have precipitated the current regression. Clinical data revealed her husband had died in the recent past, suggesting that loss of a dependency figure may have precipitated the depressive reaction. More evidence on depression, its degree and dynamics could be found in the other projective devices.

Figure 5 is rotated which, in addition to strengthening previous inferences about the meaning of rotations, suggests feelings of inadequacy. The masculine symbolism of this design may more specifically suggest that she views males as inadequate. This inference sheds some light on possible connotations of Design A. The male is subordinated to the female and is seen as distorted, possibly implying a belittling attitude toward males.

Figure 6 nearly collides with both the margin and Figure A, suggesting short-sightedness in her planning. The sinusoidal waves are perseverated, and the angulation of the curves is sharpened. These errors are consistent with the earlier general hypothesis of ego impairments which could arise from poorly-controlled intrapsychic conflicts or organicity.

This figure reinforces the early inference that her spontaneity and flexibility are impaired. Reaction formations have previously been suggested as one of her defensive maneuvers. The constriction of Figure 6 and the relative rigidity it suggests may be the result of her attempts to control the opposite pull — that is, her initial tendency was toward expansive acting out. The compactness of Figure 6 would then imply her defensive effort to control her acting out tendencies by overly inhibiting emotional expression. The increased angulation of Figure 6 is also seen at times in states of extreme anxiety and confusion. This latter inference was strongly supported by the clinical data.

Figure 7 shows numerous errors. The leaning subpart is simplified to resemble a distorted rectangle. The upright subpart shows the loss of an angle, poor line quality and mild distortions of angles at line joinings. Overwork on the bottom of the leaning subpart suggests anxiety. Severe impairment is implied through the specific source when organic or dynamic cannot be specified with certainty. Dynamic implications include low frustration tolerance with a tendency to become impatient with solving problems and to *cut-off* a task before it is finished. This tendency was confirmed in the notes made during her performance on the Bender. She expressed extreme feelings of inadequacy and impatience in trying to copy the figures and required much support from the examiner. With the inferences of depression in mind we suggest that the possibility of suicide should be considered. At times suicide can reflect a precipitous decision to solve one's problems quickly and permanently.

Figure 8 is rotated slightly clockwise and has a distortion in the center diamond. The larger trapezoid is grossly within limits with a slight distortion in size and in the oblique angles at the right. The implications for dependency conflicts and depression seen earlier in the record receive further support from these distortions. The errors in Figure 8 were milder than in Figure 7, suggesting that she can recover from regression to some degree.

Analysis of Recall

Only two figures were recalled, and they were severely distorted. Intellectual functioning at this time at least is markedly below age expectancy. Information from the other tests and general information about her past functioning would be needed to differentiate whether this lowered performance is primarily associated with mental deficiency or psychosis. The evidence from the Bender alone could imply psychosis, mental retardation or organicity. Certain features, however, suggest a functional disorder is quite likely.

Many aspects of the record show she has developed higher level functions — that is, line quality, angulation and Gestalt are at times adequate. The fact of this variability in her functioning is one source of evidence that interference from chronic, poorly controlled conflicts is quite likely to be a major component of the inadequate functioning and suggests decompensation under stress similar to the regression found in schizophrenia.

Figure 8 is very enlarged and retains the disconnected and distorted center diamond. Dependency relationships are very likely seen as distorted and engulfing with pessimism about her ability to separate and individuate.

Figure A retains the original distortion and adds an error of joining. The size is greatly reduced compared to the copy, suggesting she was drawing back from the expansive reaction originally given to this figure. The penetration of the point of the triangle into the circle suggests that she perceives male-female relationships as painful and intrusive. The possibility that her heterosexual relationships involve some sadomasochistic orientation should be explored in diagnostic interviews.

Integration

This woman revealed markedly impaired and regressive functioning in her Bender reproductions. Severe distortions and variability of quality suggest she was experiencing severe stress with a strong possibility of confused and/or psychotic thought processes. Judgment planning and reality testing were very regressed. She appears to be using a variety of defenses which are not sufficient to prevent decompensation. Denial and reaction formation around unacceptable impulses were evident. Much immaturity of personality development was implied by the regressive trends and potential symbolism of the designs she distorted. Depression with strong unresolved dependency conflicts was a recurrent theme.

Overall she appears to be a person whose adaptive ego controls are under severe stress and whose functioning resembles that of persons with a schizophrenic disorder. These general impressions were well supported by other clinical information.

Comment

This Bender record demonstrates how the reproductions reflect the functioning of an individual with a relatively severe decompensation of personality. The process of interacting with the examiner, controlling one's imagination, thoughts and reality testing in order to carry out the goal-directed tasks set by the Bender requires a relatively mature ego capable of conflict-free adaptive functioning. Where these functions have either not developed or where the impact of some type of stress interferes and brings about distortions and regressions the Bender reproductions will tend to show a drop in quality.

Since whatever interferes with adaptive ego controls can cause a drop in the efficiency of performance on the Bender, differential diagnosis can only be suggestive of trends. In the present case many indications of severe impairments in ego functioning were evident and were later confirmed by other information. However, such adaptive impairments can have many different etiologic bases, including psychosis, organicity and/or mental deficiency.

The indications of psychosis were more prominent in the present case because of the evidence of higher level potential and the variability in performance. In other words, what could be seen from this Bender record was that at times she could function close to an age-appropriate level. This evidence, together with the bizarre quality of some of the distortions, more strongly suggested a psychotic disorder than a disorder involving organicity or mental deficiency.

CASE: 09

AGE: 39

SEX: Male

Analysis of Copy

The high degree of compactness of the designs stands out as the general style of this man. Both the reduced size of all of the designs and the way the designs are cramped together suggest an extreme degree of constrictedness, withdrawal and suspiciousness. The lack of variation in sequence suggests he has a rigid, inflexible approach to his problems of living. The first impression was borne out by the clinical observation that he was grandiose, delusional, suspicious and seclusive prior to testing.

The figures appear to march down the center of the page. It's as though he looks neither right nor left as he narrowly pursues a goal. He very likely has a high degree of narcissism, placing himself and his needs in the center of his thoughts and actions. At the same time he is extremely anxious in that he fears an open and trusting relationship with the environment. This type of interaction with the relatively neutral testing situation is most apt to be found in persons who lack basic trust and who deny and project

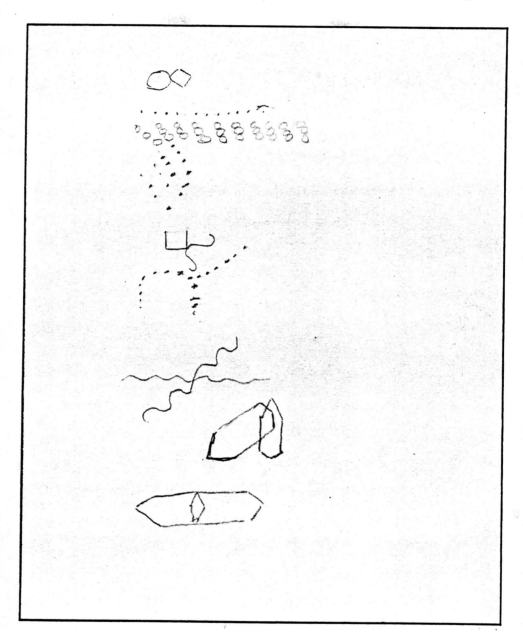

Case 09, Adult Copy

Case 09, Adult Recall

their own unacceptable hostile or aggressive impulses onto others. These characteristics, when considered with evidence of delusions and paranoid ideation, suggest he was experiencing a paranoid reaction to intrapsychic or reality stresses at the time of the testing.

Turning to the individual designs, we note that Figure A shows some line quality and closure difficulties. The circle was drawn in two parts and the square was executed with two disconnected subparts. There is a rigidity and stiltedness implied in the lack of spontaneous, continuous motion. This feature reinforces the general impression of inflexibility and lack of spontaneity in his approach to life. Further evidence of flattening of affect is seen in the reduced curvature of Figure 4 and Figure 6. There is a strong suggestion in these converging themes that he is a person who is quite isolated and withdrawn.

A mild joining error is seen at the point where the square joins the circle, resulting in an absorption of the point of the square. A similar joining problem occurs on Design 8, suggesting that close, interdependent relationships are a source of anxiety for him. There is also a possibility that separation and individuation is not clear or firm for him with a moderate tendency to blur the differences between himself and important other persons. This is similar to persons who have never fully resolved early symbiotic relationships. The symbiotic connotations of Design A further suggest that he may tend to set up symbiotic heterosexual relationships. The disconnectedness of the square implies that his masculine identity is not firm or he feels that males are somehow deficient.

Figure 1 is grossly within limits except for size which has already been generally interpreted. The line over the last dot is not interpretable as the examiner's notes did not include any comment on this feature. If it was an additional elaboration we would suspect an overactive imagination and suspect the possibility of easy withdrawal into fantasy often found with introverted and/or psychotic individuals. The Rorschach would help assess the degree and quality of imagination and the adequacy of reality testing.

Figure 2 begins with a counterclockwise rotation which then is corrected. There is a possibility that he tends to act out at times but then reconsiders and acts with better judgment. The tendency toward acting out is also seen in the subtle slashing of some of the dots in Figures 3 and 5. His general withdrawal and constriction could be a defense against the impulse to act out aggressively. The rigidity of his personality makeup implies that he may at times break under stress and lose control over the rejected impulses. Clinical data were consistent with this hypothesis. He had a history of recent recurrent episodes of destructive violence.

In Design 3 a mild tendency toward loss of control is evident as the length of time he stays with a task increases. This is suggestive of further evidence that the control of aggressive and hostile impulses may be an area of conflict for him. Information from the Rorschach and Thematic Apperception Test would help clarify the manner in which he copes with his aggressiveness.

Figure 4 shows a slight change in angulation of the curved subpart, suggesting that gratification of oral dependent needs may be an area which arouses anxiety for him.

The distortion of the dots in Figure 5 to small slashes has the same implications as in Figure 3, i.e. impatience and hostility which are controlled with effort. The number of dots is inaccurate, suggesting that in spite of the appearance of compulsiveness in the rigid sequence, he is at times careless and unobservant of detail. The accuracy of his perceptions, and his capacities for analysis and synthesis should be checked against Picture Completion, Picture Arrangement and Block designs in the WAIS and F+%, W and D in the Rorschach for more detail on this hypothesis.

Figure 6 shows an error of perseveration in the number of sine waves of the horizontal subpart. Angulation is flattened and line quality is slightly irregular. The main impression is that he was too constricted to allow free flowing motions which reinforces earlier impressions of high anxiety, withdrawal and a tendency to suppress overt expressions of emotion. Analysis of the reaction to color on the Rorschach would help give insight into how he handles his emotions and the degree of flatness of affect.

Figure 7 has a marked discrepancy in size between the two subparts. The dependent, leaning figure is much larger than the vertical supporting figure, suggesting the dependent needs of this man are felt to be much greater than can be gratified by the persons on whom he depends. A history of drug abuse makes this hypothesis at least tenable. Often persons who have experienced inadequate early parenting and who have been unable to get basic nurturant needs met will feel their demands are insatiable and greater than reality can fulfill. Historical material from the patient and informants in his family should be sought to clarify the nature of early deprivations, separations, traumas and the type of role he was assigned in the family system.

Figure 8 again shows the enlargement of the containing (parenting or mothering) trapezoid as compared to the diamond within which is further evidence of an exaggeration of dependency relationships in his imagery. The lack of connectedness of lines and integration of the diamond suggests he feels dependency figures are not soundly structured and dependable. The disconnectedness could also imply carelessness which was postulated earlier and/or anxieties and apprehensions about interpersonal relationships.

Analysis of Recall

The same basic trends continue in the recall as in the copy. He hugs the margin, clutching his designs close to each other in a rigid order. When left to his own resources he appears even more fearful and withdrawn than when he is under guidance. The figures are even smaller in size, implying heightened distrust and anxiety.

He recalled few figures, suggesting that the general constriction in his personality also inhibits his memory. The degree of his imaginativeness should be checked against the A%, R, M and content to the Rorschach. If the hypothesis of impoverished imagination were supported, the basis of the deficiency should be sought in the Rorschach and elsewhere in the test battery.

Figure 1 was essentially accurate except for the size, which was reduced. There is a suggestion of increasing tension with successful efforts at control as the dots became larger and turned into squiggle marks.

Figure 5 was simplified and reduced in size. The quality of the dots became blurred and ran together. The figure almost collided with Figure 1. The mounting tension noted in Figure 1 was beginning to get out of control and was impairing his foresight and judgment as he impatiently and angrily completed the task.

Figure 7 shows an interesting shift in emphasis. The two subparts became equal in size and were placed in parallel. The quality of lines and connectedness of both figures were poor. There is a strong possibility that when he relies on his own memory and imagination, distortions occur in his conception of relationships between objects. The distinctness and the separation-individuation of identities between individuals become blurred. This feature reinforces the hypotheses on the copy that he has inadequately resolved basic developmental issues of separation and individuation.

Often there is an even more specific possibility associated with this type of distortion. His sexual identity may very well be unclear or insecure, and he may have a potential for latent homosexuality. In the clinical management of this man the therapist should be alert to the possibility of homosexual panic as well as the larger issues of ego development, including sexual identity and separation-individuation issues.

Integration

This is the picture of a man who is highly constricted, withdrawn and flat in affect. Current stresses in his life could be precipitating some of these reactions, however the mode of the reaction very likely reflects lifelong, ingrained styles of defense involving fearfulness and suspiciousness of others. Usually persons showing this type of reaction have not experienced early object relations that were gratifying or that promoted trust, self-confidence and feelings of adequacy.

Recurrent themes in the record suggest that dependency relationships and angry feelings concerning unmet dependency needs are a source of anxiety for him. Separation and individuation issues are prominent with implications for an unclear sexual identity. More specifically, there is some reason to wonder about latent homosexual trends and the possibility of homosexual panic in the clinical management of this man.

His controls and capacity for flexible adaptation are rigid and brittle with a tendency for him to break at times under stress and lose control over his aggressive impulses.

These major hypotheses were quite consistent with clinical evidence except for the inference of latent homosexuality. There was no information available to support or reject this latter inference.

Comment

This man's Bender provided a variation on the general theme of withdrawal and constrictedness with paranoid implications seen also in Case 02. In many ways these two people shared important major personality trends, defenses and dynamics.

The Bender, however, can give clues about unique and subtle aspects of the personality important for planning the treatment of the person. A careful study of Case 02 and Case 09 should help the reader see both how these persons were similar and important ways in which they were different. Using the basic texts recommended in the "Introduction," the reader can quite possibly go beyond our interpretations and find ways to refine the understanding of these two individuals to an even greater degree than we have presented. It has been our experience that this type of effort is very instructive in gaining a working knowledge of Bender interpretation.

CASE: 10
AGE: 29
SEX: Male

Analysis of Copy

Disorganization, expansive loss of boundaries and disintegration of Gestalt in this record give the impression that this man is in an acute state of distress. Decompensation marked by high, agitated anxiety and/or confusional state appears to be occurring

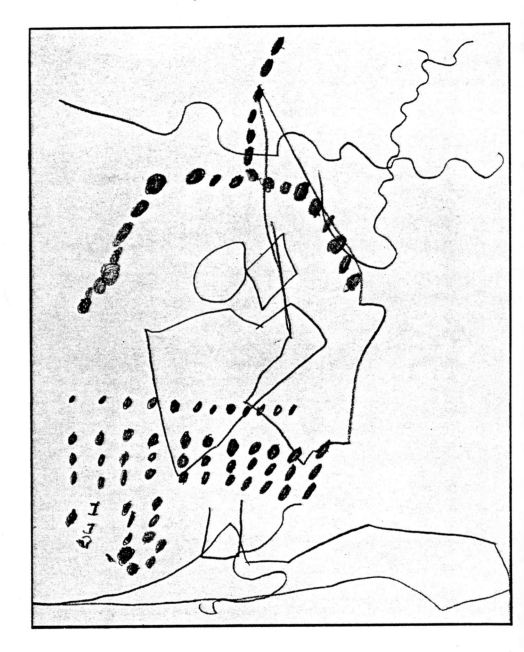

Case 10, Adult Copy, First Testing

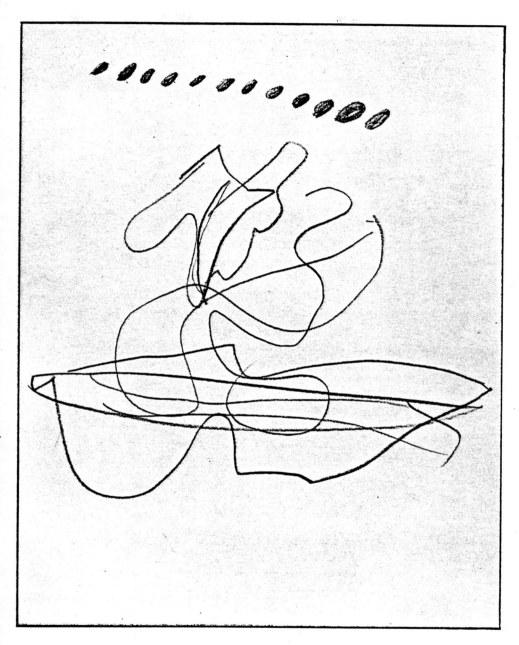

Case 10, Adult Recall, First Testing

in his functioning and reality adaptation. Extreme variations in the size of the figures suggest wide variability in functioning very likely associated with severe ambivalence and heightened intrapsychic conflicts.

The many collisions, including overrunning the edge of the page for Figure 8, indicate extreme intolerance for boundaries, indifference to the demands of reality, extreme impulsivity, lack of foresight and planning and difficulty with figure-ground relationships. Judgment and reality testing are extremely poor. Interpersonal relations would be expected to be marked by an indifference to social conventions, high egocentrism (seen in the location of first drawing) and overt acting out of anxieties.

Gross disorganization of personality is seen in the disintegration of Gestalt and the unpredictable order of the designs. He began the task attempting to gain order using a vertical direction and the edge of the page for Figures 1, 2 and 3. Thereafter he placed the designs with only the most minimal attention given to adequate spacing. He was still reality testing to some degree as seen in his efforts to introduce order and in the fact that most of the designs were recognizable in shape even though distorted.

A progressive deterioration is seen in the increasing distortion of size and Gestalt following Figure 4 which suggests that his capacity for active goal-directed concentration and attention was very limited at the time of testing. Persons in acute states, whether from psychotic crises, drugs or organicity, will sometimes react to the fatigue of concentrated effort with a drop in reality testing. A similar phenomenon can be observed in the Rorschach records of some schizophrenics, i.e. a drop in quality of percepts and/or increasingly gory or bizarre content on the later ink blots as compared to the blots earlier in the series. The progressive deterioration gives further evidence of ego impairments in this man's functioning and suggests a severe regression.

Clinical information was consistent with these overall impressions from the Bender. He was highly agitated and anxious, showing extremely poor judgment and disregard for social boundaries such as bursting into doctor's offices without appointments and reporting a delusion of having been shot. His premorbid personality had been marked by strong clinging dependency and a history of psychiatric hospitalizations. In many ways he resembled an inadequate personality during states of remission. The precipitating event for the present crisis involved conflicts with persons on whom he was extremely dependent and the threat of impending hospitalization for a physical condition that had resulted from a lack of adequate self-care.

The analysis of the individual designs can help provide leads to what may be involved in this man's distress and indications of where strengths may lie that might help him reintegrate.

Figure A was placed in the center of the page, a position often taken by narcissistic and self-centered persons who judge the world in terms of their own needs. Both the square and the circle are slightly distorted, although at this point he was able to integrate the subparts much better than later in the record. He was able to maintain the goal-directed effort involving imaging, visual-motor coordination and integration for at least a short period of time. The increased angulation of the design suggests some hostility may penetrate his interpersonal relations.

After beginning at the center of the page he shifts to the margin, suggesting an immature need to cling to others for support and structure. Design A indicates the high anxiety and tension he was experiencing as seen in the enlarged dots. He perseverates this style of forming the dots in Figures 2, 3 and 5. Persons who have excessive degrees of internal tension without adequate channels for discharge often tend to give enlarged dots.

Figure 2, in addition to the already-noted blackened circles, shows a tendency toward a clockwise rotation, suggesting depression and/or a flattening of affect. This tendency is also seen in Figure 3 and Figure 6 which reinforces the notion that there is some depression.

Design 3 is more disorganized than the first three figures with a peculiar distortion of the dots in the second column from the left. The examiner did not inquire about the meaning of these dots which look like capital I's, so there is no way to know if they had special symbolic significance for the person. At the very least they are a marked departure from dots and reflect a gross distortion of the design, suggesting the possibility that an overly-active fantasy or an autistic process may have been occurring.

The third and fourth columns of Design 3 reflect progressively greater disorganization of Gestalt with simplification and angulation changes. There is a possibility that the aggressive connotations of this design aroused conflicts around the expression of unacceptable impulses which interfered with his ability to carry the task to completion and integrate the separate dots properly. The tension seen in the enlarged dots may very well involve suppressed aggressive impulses which were aroused by the demand for concentrated attention but which he feared expressing toward the examiner. The clinical information that he had a delusion he was shot is consistent with the inference that denied and projected hostility is one component of his personality and dynamics.

Figure 4 is distorted in size and Gestalt, suggesting anxieties around oral dependent themes. There is a strong possibility he conceptualizes nurturing relationships as not being very gratifying. There is a tendency to perseverate the sinusoidal wave, a characteristic also seen in Figure 6, suggesting a manic state reflected in poor ability to modulate emotional arousal which leads to an inattention to details and reality limits. When he begins a continuous activity he has difficulty stopping. Since perseveration occurred only on designs with the sinusoidal waves, there is a likelihood that the emotional determinants are prominent.

Perseveration has high loadings as a discriminating factor for organicity. However, the pressure of poorly-controlled drives in psychotic states can also lead to a tendency to be repetitious. Curvature difficulty is a sensitive indicator of emotional disturbance. The combination of increased curvature indicating overly-active emotionality along with decreased curvature or flattening suggests his emotional controls are chaotic. He attempts to cope with his emotions first by constriction and flattening and then by acting out only to revert to inhibition again elsewhere. None of his defenses or ego adaptive mechanisms were working very effectively at the time of this testing.

Figure 5 is grossly enlarged which reflects an expansiveness following Figure 4. Conflicts and anxieties aroused by Figure 4 may have contributed to the high level of drive and loss of control seen in Figure 5. Other factors such as the symbolic value of Figure 5 and/or the tendency for fatigue to erode his ego functions as noted earlier may also have been operating in this reproduction. If the symbolic masculine connotations did arouse the intense conflict and anxiety, then the inference would be that he has severe conflicts concerning his masculine identity. The huge size further suggests a masculine protest, an effort to feel and appear strong and adequate when he feels devastatingly impotent and inadequate. Clinical observation suggested this latter inference was quite tenable as he was overtly and inappropriately seductive toward the female examiner.

Figure 6 has largely been discussed in terms of perseveration and curvature difficulties previously. The emphasis on the left lateral aspect of the figure has connotations for withdrawal tendencies and a turning toward fantasy. The fact of his delusional state makes this hypothesis seem quite tenable. The Rorschach would provide further information about the quantity and quality of his imagination and reality testing.

Figure 7 is grossly distorted in size, suggesting both a continuation of his loss of control and expansiveness and also implying organicity and/or severe interpersonal difficulties. The Gestalt is lost with only a faint semblance of two intertwined objects which implies a gross breakdown in capacity for image formation, frustration tolerance and goal-directed visual-motor control.

The simplification, expansiveness and severe distortion continues in Figure 8, suggesting further evidence of a progressive deterioration in his capacity for sound judgment and reality level adaptive functioning.

Analysis of Recall

Only three figures were recalled, which is below average for adults of average intelligence, suggesting his memory was impaired.

The progressive deterioration seen in the copy continued and increased in the recall. Figure 1 is more expansive and shows the struggle with a high level of anxiety and/or chaotic drives. The downward rotation is suggestive of a depressive mood which increased as he was left to function more on his own resources.

The remaining two figures are barely recognizable, and impulse control became so disorganized that he finally deteriorated into a scribble, no longer trying to tolerate the frustration and tension of reality testing, impulse modulation and goal-directed adaptive functioning. The Gestalt is so confused and distorted that simplified and distorted versions of Figure 7 and Figure 8 can hardly be identified. The blob-like form beneath Design 1 resembles the distorted copy of Figure 7. The horizontal scribbles resemble the distorted copy of Figure 8. Reality testing, judgment and impulse control have obviously slipped to a point where the productions resemble the scribbles of a preschool child.

Integration

This man is in a state of personality decompensation where his conflicts, anxieties and impulses have overcome the ego adaptive functions, resulting in extremely poor reality testing and judgment. Frustration tolerance, impulse delay and capacity for integration are severely reduced.

He is able to function for short periods of time with some integration, but this quickly gives way to the pressure of his drives, affect and conflicts. Interpersonal relations are markedly distorted with extreme indifference to the boundaries of reality including social conventions.

The rudiments of premorbid personality organization are hinted at in those designs that remain relatively intact. In a structured situation he can still cope to a minimal degree. In more open, ambiguous situations he has few resources for integrating himself, and he quickly becomes chaotic and confused in his approach to solving problems or maintaining goal direction.

There is little doubt about the acute severity of his regression. The etiology of the precipitating stress could not be known from the Bender alone. Clinical information suggests he was in a state of panic over rejections he was experiencing in his dependency relationships, and he was also facing a major physical illness. Acute brain syndromes and toxic conditions could also be a primary determining factor in such severe personality decompensation. The premorbid picture was that of an inadequate personality with borderline psychotic features. Clinical follow-up suggested that the stress of perceived rejections and the threat of an impending serious health problem overwhelmed his tenuous reality adjustment and precipitated the acute crisis seen in his Bender reproductions.

Comment

This record provides a rich source of data concerning the method in which the task set by the Bender reflects personality and ego functioning. In spite of the extremely chaotic and regressed reproductions, clues remained about his personality that gave an understanding of him as a unique person. He was experiencing extreme levels of stress which overwhelmed a chronically tenuous personality integration.

Nevertheless, the suggestions of strong and chronic feelings of masculine inadequacy, pervasive and insatiable dependency needs and a tendency toward a narcissistic and egocentric approach to the world were stable components of his personality during states of remission.

The Six Week Follow Up Retest

A six-week follow up testing was done after a period of chemotherapy with antipsychotic drugs. The copy and recall of that retest are presented next. The analysis of the follow-up will depart from the analysis of the first testing. Instead of analyzing his personality directly the emphasis will be on a comparison of the two sets of data. The first was taken during an acute crisis, and the second was administered during a state of relative reintegration.

Analysis of Copy of Retest

The contrast between the Bender taken during his acute crisis and the follow-up testing clearly reflects the increased personality integration that has occurred. The figures of the retest are all recognizable even though serious ego deficiencies remain.

The expansiveness is far better controlled and reality boundaries are much better observed. Figures 6 and 8 are the only collisions as compared to excessive collisions in the acute state. The degree of improvement in ego controls and reintegration is also seen in the improved sequence of the reproductions. He was, at this time, planning ahead more adequately and organizing and

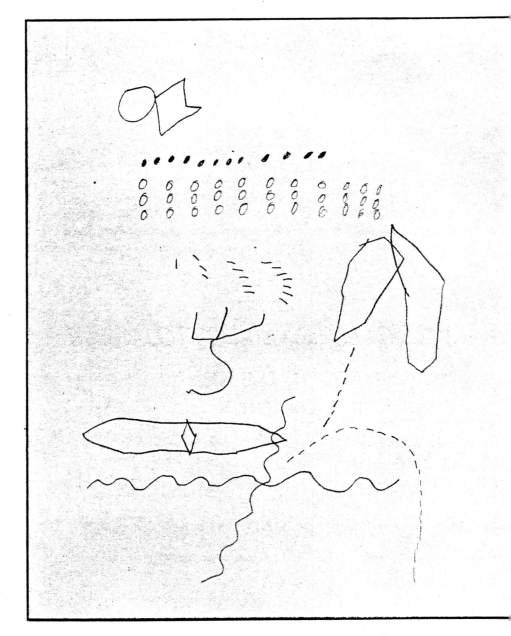

Case 10, Adult Copy, Second Testing

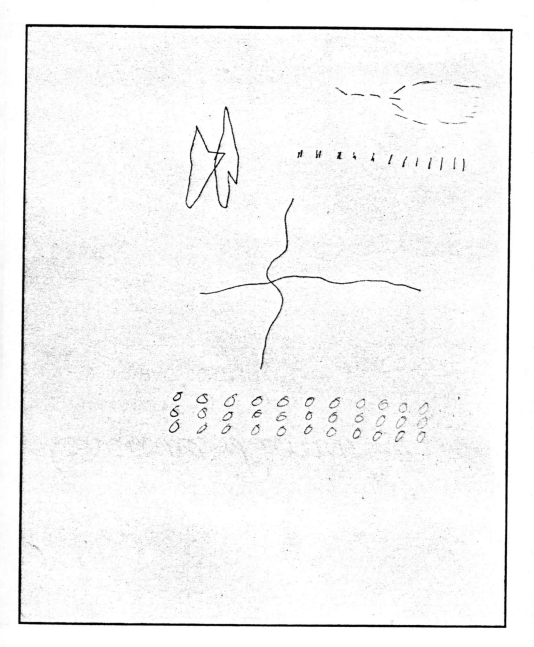

Case 10, Adult Recall, Second Testing

ordering his work with much more regard for the boundaries of the page. This was paralleled in his behavior by a better controlled and more orderly approach to his interpersonal relationships. His organization remains brittle, however, resulting in disorganization when he has to cope with change as is seen in the disorganization that occurred after Figure 5 when he had to change direction at the bottom of the page.

Although line quality and angulation difficulties remain, they are present in a much lesser degree than during the acute stage. Angulation errors on Figures A, 7 and 8 and curvature difficulties seen in Figures 4 and 6 could be caused by either cerebral dysfunction or emotional conflicts. Information from within the test battery should be sought here to help make a more precise differential diagnosis. There is a sufficient degree of impairment to suggest that a neurological examination should also be recommended. Signs of organicity in the projective techniques should be carefully weighed as further evidence of intracranial pathology.

An examination of each of the individual designs in the retest can help provide clues concerning personality trends and components that may become prominent in a state of remission.

Figure A reveals a size distortion. Both subparts are diminished in size as compared to the stimulus. This suggests that a pulling back from the environment is an aspect of how he has coped with his earlier tendencies toward chaotic overexpansiveness. Further evidence of personality constriction is also seen in the tighter clustering of all the designs. Figure A was placed in a more usual position in this retest, suggesting a shift toward less egocentrism and self-preoccupation.

The distortion of the square of Figure A suggests he may have chronic feelings of masculine deficiency. Support for this hypothesis is given by the exaggerated size of Figure 5 and the displaced phallic-like extension of Figure 5 suggesting compensation for feelings of inadequacy. The previously noted seductiveness and clinging dependent behavior suggests that his masculine identity may very well be a source of chronic anxiety for him. Strong underlying feelings of inadequacy and feelings of impotence can contribute to carelessness in achievement and may also have been an aspect of this distortion.

Figure 1 is markedly reduced in size compared to the original. The blacked-in dots suggest strong tensions continue but to a lesser degree than before. Unevenness in the horizontal plane suggests a shaky level of ego integration. Efforts to control the inner tensions and conflicts reduce his capacity for sustained realistic, goal-directed effort.

Figure 2 shows marked improvement. The circles are essenially correct suggesting he can now function at least for some periods of time at a relatively effective, reality-oriented level. The columns of circles are rotated slightly clockwise. This suggests that his depression remains but to a lesser degree. He has difficulty carrying out a task and soon begins to feel a depletion of his coping resources. Sometimes this type of reaction is found in emotionally-deprived and borderline persons who complain that the demands of testing exhaust or drain them. Clinical observation would help confirm this inference.

Figure 3 is much more contained and the units are better integrated than before. The excessive, unchanneled tensions have become translated into more highly controlled hostile slashes. The downward rotation is further evidence of a depressive trend and/or flattening of affect. There is a distinct possibility that the aggressive connotations of Figure 3 aroused anxiety about his own aggressive impulses. The flattening seen in the rotation and in the rounding of the angulation suggests that he attempts to cope with his aggression by suppression. However, hostile feelings remain and are expressed in the impatient slashing of the dots.

Figure 4 is improved over the original reproduction. The curved subpart shows increased angulation, poor line quality and displacement of point of contact. He very likely has difficulty accepting his oral dependent needs and sets up peripheral relationships with nurturing figures. Close relationships would be expected to cause him anxiety although he has not entirely withdrawn from human relationships. The peripheral connections in Figure 7 reinforce the inference that he has interpersonal anxieties but still wishes to remain in contact with others and has not totally withdrawn. Schizoid individuals who have strong basic distrust of human relationships but who also have some continuing desire for relatedness will sometimes reveal this conflict in the peripheral and displaced connections between subparts of the compound designs. Relationships are seen by them as dangerous and destructive.

Figure 5 is much more contained than the original, showing again how much calmer and better integrated he was at the time of the retest. The extreme unchanneled tension seen in the original has given way to a much more contained figure with dots turned into dashes. This suggests as in Figure 3 a suppression of impatience and hostility with the further implication that his heterosexual relationships may be marked by hostile feelings or interactions.

The curved part of Figure 5 has additional units (perseveration) which also occurred in Figure 6. The emotional implications of the curved figures could contribute to perseveration. Cerebral dysfunction is often associated with perseveration. In his acute state the emotional turmoil was a very likely cause of the perseveration. However, in the calmer, more integrated state of the retest situation the hypothesis of central nervous system dysfunction should be considered.

Figure 6 has been partially discussed in terms of perseveration and curvature difficulties. The penetration of Figure 6 into Figure 5 could have many implications. The most basic possibility is an indifference to boundaries which was discussed previously. At times the aggressiveness reflected in the defiance of boundaries is associated with suicide. The projective techniques as well as clinical data should be scrutinized for signs of suicidal ideation or tendency.

Figure 7 has largely been discussed in relation to problems of angulation and interpersonal implications. Much improvement from the original is evident. The symbolic connotations of dependency in this figure suggest he has not experienced early relationships that were gratifying or that built his trust in people. The conception of relationships between dependent and nurturant figures is one marked by painful distance where objects touch only by distortion of their own structure. This inference, if correct, suggests that he views relationships with others as painful, frustrating and resulting in destruction of his personal integrity. Clinical observation was consistent with this formulation.

Figure 8 collides with Figure 6 suggesting in part that the sustained effort at performing a concentrated task was exceeding his controls. He was beginning to ignore reality boundaries and failing to look ahead and plan adequately. He has shown marked progress from the original acute state but still has deficiencies in reality testing, judgment and self-control.

Numerous errors occurred on Figure 8. Angles were rounded or distorted, the center diamond was shrunken in size and overran at the points of joining. Line quality was poor. The significance of these errors collectively is that he is careless in carrying out the activity and very likely disregards the reality demands of the physical and social environment in his everyday adaptation. As compared to the original testing, marked progress has been made, and this shows that he has not only reintegrated to a large extent but has also been able to sustain this level of compensation throughout the copy phase of the test. This is a sign that his reintegration was beginning to become fairly firm.

Many chronic deficiencies remain as seen in the copy phase. He was still functioning at a level where much external ego support and guidance were necessary to help him cope.

Analysis of the Recall of the Retest

The recall reflects the marked progress toward personality integration seen in the copy. Five figures were recalled as compared to three on the first testing which suggests that his premorbid level of intelligence was probably at least in the average range. As in the copy phase of the retest, the degree of reality testing, adequacy of judgment and planning, and resources for coping (memory, self-control, emotional integration, cognitive functioning) are all much improved over the acute phase although still deficient in many respects as compared to average adult functioning.

Figure 2 was reproduced relatively accurately but with mild clockwise rotations which suggests that some flattening of affect may be present. Figure 6 reinforces the notion of flattened affect since the spontaneous flow of the curves is eliminated, suggesting that the price of his reintegration is the suppression of feeling and emotion.

Figure 1 suggests that the unchanneled tensions seen in the copy find a more constricted expression of hostility (squiggle lines and dashes) when he is left on his own. There is a further possibility that he starts a task trying to suppress aggressive impulses and gradually begins to lose control the longer he stays with the task (the dashes become increasingly larger). Similarly, Figure 5 converts dots to dashes, suggesting he has a pervasive and chronic hostility. The counterclockwise rotation is sometimes found with tendencies to act out fantasies and impulses. The masculine symbolism of Figure 5 suggests he may conceive of masculinity in terms of hostile, aggressive acts. Of course, these inferences would have to be verified against other testing data and general information.

Figure 7 reveals gross distortions, suggesting that his memory trace was inaccurate. When he must rely on his own cognitive abilities he is likely to reveal gross distortions at times.

The extreme difficulty seen with the angles suggests the possibility of central nervous system dysfunction. This was also seen in various facets of the copy phase. If emotional ambivalence and conflict are causative factors in the distortion of Figure A, then it is highly likely that he views interpersonal relations as extremely frustrating and destructive. The sharpened angle of the dependent figure penetrating the supporting vertical figure of Design 8 implies that he tends to set up sadomasochistic relationships with people on whom he depends. Clinical observations suggested that he did tend to develop parasitic dependency relationships which were so irritating that he ultimately became the victim of rejections. No further evidence was available to help clarify the presence of organicity.

Integration of Retest

The retest clearly indicates that this man had begun reintegrating after an acute episode of panic with accompanying personality decompensation and psychotic regression.

The price of the reintegration, as judged from the Bender, was in part a forfeiting of spontaneous emotions with some withdrawal and flattening of affect. In the calmer state the Bender very likely reflects more closely his premorbid personality which resembles that of an inadequate personality with potential for psychotic regression under stress.

Judgment and reality testing improved markedly but remained below expectancy for mature adult functioning. He has chronic, poorly-controlled conflicts, anxieties and tensions remaining. Sexual identity is very poorly established and issues of separation and individuation remain prominent. Judgment, forethought and planning are at an immature level. This man would be expected to need continued ego-supportive maintenance. Other testing data and clinical observation were consistent with these major hypotheses.

Comment

Many basic aspects of the relationship between Bender reproductions, personality and ego functioning were illustrated dramatically by this case. The demand characteristics of the task for integrated cognitive functioning, visual-motor control and reality adaptation can be easily seen in reproductions when an acute phase is compared to a state of remission in the same person.

Of special interest are the subtle variations seen in more integrated states as compared to the extreme variations in the acute state. For example, extreme, unchanneled tension is reflected in the copy of Figure 1 for the acute (original) as compared to the more contained copy of Figure 1 in the retesting which still, nevertheless, reflects a high degree of tension.

In some instances such as Figures 6, 7 and 8 the uncontrolled and overpowering state of emotional arousal appeared to act somewhat like an amplifier on premorbid personality trends. Similar types of difficulties were seen in these figures in both the acute and retesting phases with the difference being that in the acute phase both the size of the figures and the degree of the distortion were greater than in the state where reintegration was occurring.

Another feature of interest in this record is that clues to this man's premorbid personality can be seen even during his acute episode. For example, the suggestion of conflicts and anxiety concerning the dependency themes of Figures 4 and 7 were evident even when he was enduring a relatively severe personality decompensation. Similarly, the suggestion of feelings of impotence and overcompensation for feelings of masculine inadequacy were evident in Figure 5 during the acute phase and remained prominent although much more contained on the retesting.

The reader is encouraged to search for more comparisons between the acute phase and the retesting phase. This will help to illustrate both the cognitive and personality basis of Bender interpretation in general and more specifically how the Bender, even when administered in acute states, can help the examiner to understand a person more fully. Such increased knowledge and understanding of Bender interpretation techniques are of great importance in making suggestions for the management of the treatment process.

Chapter 3

INTERPRETATION OF CHILD
AND ADOLESCENT PROTOCOLS

CASE: 01

AGE: 10

SEX: Male

Analysis of Copy

MANY features of this record immediately suggest that this boy is not functioning at an entirely age-appropriate level. There are numerous general indications of some form of ego impairment and/or emotional disturbance which will be discussed in more detail later. For the moment we notice greater distortions of Gestalt than would be expected for his age level, variability in use of space and order of placement, and deviation in size and line quality. All of these suggest a disturbance in his functioning and adaptation. This first impression was consistent with information from the examiner that this child was attending a special school for children with learning disabilities. Presenting complaints included sporadic uncooperative class behavior, high anxiety about achievement and a tendency to have psychosomatic concerns.

Turning first to examine his work methods we notice that Figure A is placed in a relatively conventional position suggesting he has incorporated some of the general social expectancies. Information from the Rorschach, especially the number of populars would be of interest in relation to this inference. Placement of the other figures on the page is disorganized which is very likely related to a similar lack of organization in his personality and adaptive abilities.

He has some rudimentary organization, largely selecting empty spaces to place his figures similar to the technique of a younger

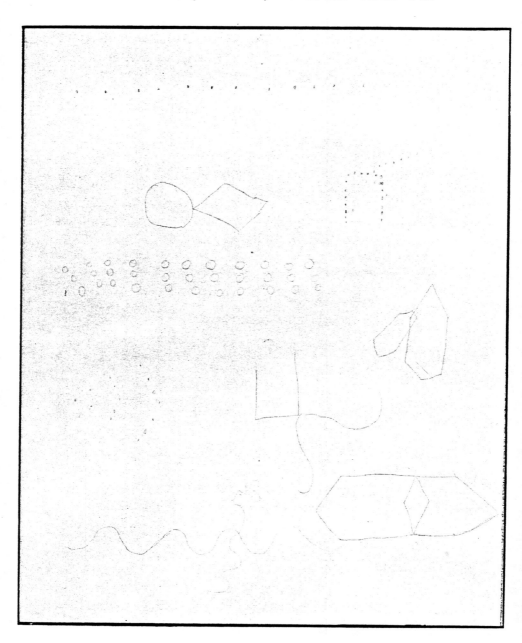

Case 01, Child Copy

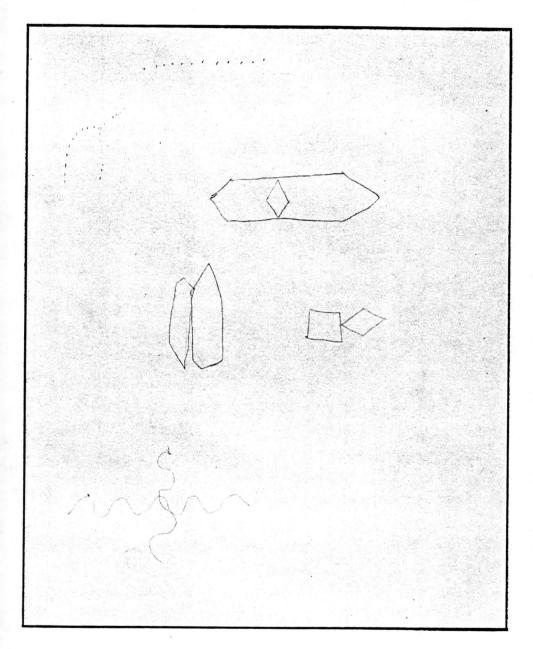

Case 01, Child Recall

child. He plans sufficiently to avoid collisions with the other designs although there is a tendency toward collision in some instances. He has apparently incorporated a sufficient degree of individuation and identity to respect the boundaries between himself and others. The overall quality of his planning is less than would be expected for his age. He is not likely to do very well if he is left dependent upon his own organization ability. This could be one factor related to his reported anxieties about achievement since poor planning and forethought are apt to lead to failures in achievement.

There are indications of some partially controlled and compensated hostile attitudes in his tendency to arrange figures in an ascending order (Figs. 1, 5 and 7) from time to time. Usually this tendency is accompanied by hostile negativistic attitudes toward authorities and often is related to tendencies toward withdrawal. The expansive use of space is further evidence of some tendencies to act out aggressive and rebellious feelings. Further evidence of acting out tendencies is seen in the size deviations. Five figures or subparts were larger than standard (using Clawson, 1962, p. 145) and three were smaller than standard expectancy. Such variability is often associated with conflicts concerning impulse modulation. Unevenness in size is usually associated with low frustration tolerance and a tendency to have labile behavior with a precarious adjustment.

The decrease in figure size is sometimes associated with internalization of anxiety and somatic complaints. This is consistent with reports that this boy complained of backaches without evidence of a physical basis for the discomfort. The way he handled color on the Rorschach would further clarify these hypotheses. Uneven figure size is often accompanied by strong reactions to external and emotional stimulation which is often seen in strong reactions to color on the Rorschach.

Turning next to examine what the individual figures may reveal we notice that Figure A has numerous moderate distortions. The square is expanded laterally and the right-hand angle was at first not brought to closure. He completed the closure by addition of a small angle. The left part of the square is lengthened to make contact with the circle. This suggests anxieties concerning contacts with females and at the same time a continued motivation to maintain such contact even though it may be a source of stress for him.

The closure difficulty contains two possible inferences for this boy. First, he may have feelings about his own completeness or feelings of defectiveness. There is a strong possibility he feels quite inadequate and somehow deficient. Masculine identification may be a source of stress for him. His treatment of Figure 5, increasing the angulation and decreasing the size as well as spontaneously redoing the figure further supports the inference that his masculine identity or the masculine role is a source of anxiety for him.

The second distinct possibility is that he is very fearful of interpersonal relations. Children with emotional deprivation or children who have not had satisfying relationships with significant adults will sometimes reveal fears of closeness in this manner. Joining difficulties seen in Figures 4 and 6 give further evidence that in regard to interpersonal relations he very likely does experience anxiety that is moderately beyond average and probably relates to feelings of inadequacy and self-doubt.

Figure 1 is grossly within limits, showing that his development and/or functioning is not even. In some areas he has progressed to an age-appropriate level, but in others he is less advanced. The scatter of subtest scores in the Wechsler Intelligence Scale for Children would help further delineate his pattern of strengths and weaknesses in intellectual functioning. We have noticed that records of children reflecting as much unevenness in Bender reproductions as this child shows will usually have significantly uneven WISC profiles, reflecting the trauma and blockage in their development and personality.

Figure 2 was begun with an approximately correct orientation but with a slightly greater counterclockwise rotation than the stimulus card. He then compensated and overcorrected with too great a clockwise rotation. The angulation of the columns fluctuating thereafter with the last column is essentially correct. Several hypotheses seem likely about this performance. He seems to begin a new situation or face a new problem with some regression. That is, a mild counterclockwise rotation is common for Figure 2 until ten years of age. He has the capacity to perceive accurately and correct himself with effort. The sustained effort of concentrated goal-directed activity causes him some frustration as he tries to maintain the proper vertical and horizontal orientation. Overall this figure confirms the earlier impression that he functions un-evenly.

He essentially retained the Gestalt in Figure 3 with evidence of a vertical expansion in the last column of dots. There is also some mild retrogression in the last column, i.e. two dots converted to circles. The mild tendency toward regression and/or expansive-ness has been seen previously in Figures A and 2 which gives evidence that he has a persistent tendency to regress under the stress of a goal-directed task. He struggles against his regressive tendencies and manages to maintain a fairly good level of reality testing. The adequacy of his resources for coping with stress and sustaining the frustration of goal-directed activities is open to question. The Rorschach would help gain a richer view of his personality resources and help to assess the brittleness of his defenses.

Figure 4 shows an enlargement of the vertical dimension of the open square, a joining error, a slight increase in the altitude of the sine wave, and poor coordination in line quality of the sine wave. The unevenness of the sides of the square suggests impulsiveness and low frustration tolerance. The increase in the vertical dimen-sion reinforces earlier hypotheses of conflict in regard to author-ity figures and oppositional tendencies.

The difficulty he experienced in joining the subparts of Figure 4 suggests anxieties concerning oral dependency themes. Mild psychomotor blocking is seen in the poor line quality. Hesitancy and self-doubt are implied in the poor coordination as he ap-proached the point of joining the sine wave with the rectangle. Figure A reveals a similar phenomenon in the drawing of the circle, suggesting that the joining of masculine and feminine imagery causes him some tension. The mild increase in altitude of the sine wave is thought to be associated with tendencies toward overreaction to emotional stimulation. His manner of coping with color on the Rorschach would give additional data on this latter hypothesis.

Figure 5 was begun twice. The first time the design was greatly reduced in size, indicating withdrawal tendencies under the im-pact of anxiety. A combination of inadequate anticipatory planning and overly self-critical attitudes are often associated with redrawing. Figure 6 also shows a redrawing of the vertical subpart, reinforcing the hypothesis that he does not plan ahead well and doubts his abilities to achieve. The presenting complaint that he shows anxiety about achievement in school makes these hypotheses about his redrawing tendency all the more likely.

The sketching observed in Figures 6 and 8 further supports the inferences that he tends to have strong self-doubts, intense anxiety and feelings of personal inadequacy hinted at in other areas of his productions. The size reduction of Figure 5 and the clockwise rotation of the phallic-like extension suggest feelings of impotence and inadequacy. This boy has very likely internalized a view of himself as inadequate and impotent. He tries to overcome these feelings and strives to achieve but only partially succeeds. The conflict aroused by his self-doubts and expectation of a critical attitude from others reduces his capacity to sustain goal-directed efforts. Internalization of a masculine identity is at best shaky.

Figure 6 has been partially discussed. The sketchiness, poor line quality and redrawing of the vertical subpart all suggest intense anxiety and self-doubts, very likely including hypercritical attitudes. These distortions can also be based on mild organic brain dysfunction which has been compensated. Often one impact of minimal brain dysfunction on children is to leave them with feelings of inferiority, high anxiety and expectations of failure since they are unable to compete with their peers due to impairments in perceptual-motor functioning. The signs of minimal brain dysfunction in this boy's record are minimal, and the distortions could also be the product of anxiety and personality conflicts. The scatter on the WISC and the analysis of the Rorschach would help establish a differential diagnosis.

Figure 7 has a severe size reduction in the left trapezoid suggesting intense feelings in regard to primary dependency relationships. The intertwining of the two figures is also reduced. He quite likely fears close, interdependent relationships but not to a degree that he withdraws entirely. The reduced size also suggests he feels small and inadequate in comparison to the larger, more powerful adults in his world.

Figure 8 has a size distortion in the increased width of the trapezoid, giving it a short, fat appearance which some clinicians infer as a *feminization*. Given the mounting evidence that he has feelings of inadequacy and impotence it is quite possible he has some degree of feminine identification or conflict concerning internalization of a more feminine passive role for himself.

Analysis of Recall

The recall of six figures suggests at least average intelligence. Many changes occurred in comparison to the copy phase. The figures were generally reduced in size with increased space between, implying an increase in anxiety with a tendency to withdraw from others under the impact of the anxiety. In general, more distortion is observed in the Gestalt of the figures, and one contamination occurred which suggests that when he must rely on his own resources, anxiety increases and ego functions drop in efficiency. His judgment and reality testing are not as good when he is left on his own as compared to when he can rely on the environment for structure and guidance.

Next we turn to the individual designs. We see a contamination in Figure A — that is, the combination of different parts of separate designs. The right-hand square very likely came from Design A. The left subpart cannot be clearly traced as no Bender design exactly corresponds to it. The open rectangle of Figure 4 is closest. The masculine symbolism replacing the feminine symbolism (the circle) suggests anxieties and conflicts concerning sexual identity. The specific nature of his conflict cannot be inferred from this design alone. In conjunction with Figure 7 there are implications of homosexuality. Rejection of the feminine in himself may also be implied.

Figure 1 is reduced in size although accurate. He tends to withdraw from interaction with others when he feels threatened and insecure. His self-doubt increases the more he is left on his own.

Figure 5 was redrawn, revealing his poor anticipatory planning and self-doubt. In spite of his efforts to reality test (the reworking of the design) his conflicts distort the final product with increased vertical expansion. The implication of oppositional tendencies and/or overcompensation for feelings of masculine inadequacy is strong.

Figure 6 has a size reduction and a perseveration of sine waves in the horizontal plane. The vertical plane is simplified, and difficulty is evident at the point of crossover. Distortions in his memory trace have taken place. The factor of perseveration is usually associated with organicity although it can be the product of personality functioning involving a narrow and constricted attention as he performs a task. Spontaneous and adaptive ego controls are impaired to a mild degree.

The mild counterclockwise rotation and the simplification of the vertical line suggests a tendency to act out under stress, possibly in an oppositional and/or passive aggressive fashion. The difficulty of crossover is often associated with strong friction in interpersonal relationships. The type of M on the Rorschach would provide increased information about his conception of interpersonal roles. In general, Figure 6 reflects rigidity, anxiety and acting out tendencies when he is emotionally aroused.

Figure 7 is markedly changed from the copy phase. There is relatively little interpenetration, and the figures are rotated to a nearly parallel status. These distortions suggest a lack of clarity in individuation with implications for his sexual identity. The possibility of latent homosexual trends is evident. At the very least there is an implication that his individual identity has not crystallized to an age-appropriate degree which supports the sexual implications seen in Figure A.

Integration

This young man gives the impression of a person who has a high degree of chronic anxiety related to underlying feelings of inadequacy and self-doubt.

He attempts to compensate for an internalized view of himself as a person who cannot perform well, but his efforts to achieve reach only partial success. His lack of self-confidence and view of himself as inadequate cause him to regress frequently even where he has the basic capacities to do better. His self-doubt very likely has an element of projection involved in that he expects harsh rejection from others which in part is related to his own hypercritical attitude toward himself.

Object relations are marked by tendencies to withdraw and keep his distance from others, a defensive maneuver which increases as he becomes more anxious or feels more vulnerable as at the times when he must rely more on himself. In general he has more than an expected degree of fearfulness of others, although he continues to seek contact with people in spite of his expectations of friction in relationships.

His sexual identification is less well-established than would be expected for his age. There are hints in his reproductions that he is quite unsure of his masculinity. He attempts to compensate for his feelings of inadequacy by sometimes putting on a masculine facade. His self-doubts, however, do not allow him to maintain such a facade, and he soon retreats to a more passive-dependent orientation.

Many of the features displayed by this boy both in psychomotor functions and in personality are often found in children who have minimal brain dysfunction. Only a tentative differential diagnosis can be made from the Bender alone. If he had MBD it has been compensated to a large degree, and only hints of it remain in poor line quality and the clues pointing to an ingrained view he has of himself as somehow inadequate or deficient. The stronger hypothesis would seem to be that his personality traits and chronic anxiety are the major factors contributing to the types of distortions seen in his reproductions.

Comment

This record gives an example of the types of developmental and diagnostic inferences which can be made from a Bender protocol for a child in late latency. It should be noted that the rate of visual-motor maturation as measured by the Bender is essentially similar for males and females. Koppitz (1972) and Clawson (1962) cite relevant normative data which is combined for both males and females.

The only essential difference in the interpretive process between records of boys and girls pertains to inferences about sexuality. All other inferences drawn to level of perceptual-motor development, intelligence, personality functioning and psychopathology are essentially the same for boys or girls. Inferences about sexual identity or development, of course, are drawn in the light of theory, research and clinical experience relevant for the given sex.

In the present case, inferences were drawn to the formation of the boys sexual identity and feelings about his masculinity. If this record had been produced by a girl, the inferences would have been altered accordingly.

For example, the distortions in Figure A would have been interpreted as relating to the girl's feelings about male and female sexuality. In the present case, Figure A of the copy might have been interpreted as reflecting the girl's anxieties about males and possibly a demeaning attitude toward males since the square was reproduced with greater imperfection than the circle.

Accordingly, speculations about the girl's development of a sexual identity would be made in the framework of existing theory and clinical knowledge. The basic works on the Bender cited in the "Introduction" to this book provide a rich source of interpretations for protocols produced by either males or females.

CASE: 02

AGE: 11

SEX: Male

Analysis of Copy

The most impressive feature of this Bender protocol is the use of boxes to separate the different designs. There is a strong implication that this boy uses a variety of intellectual defenses including isolation of affect and compulsivity to contain and control his impulses. The need for such rigid defenses suggests the presence of a severe disturbance which might in part be a function of approaching adolescence but which in degree is more severe than the usual adolescent reaction. At the very least the use of boxes implies rigid intellectual defenses and often involves strong feelings of inadequacy.

This initial impression from the Bender record was consistent with information from the boy's school and information from

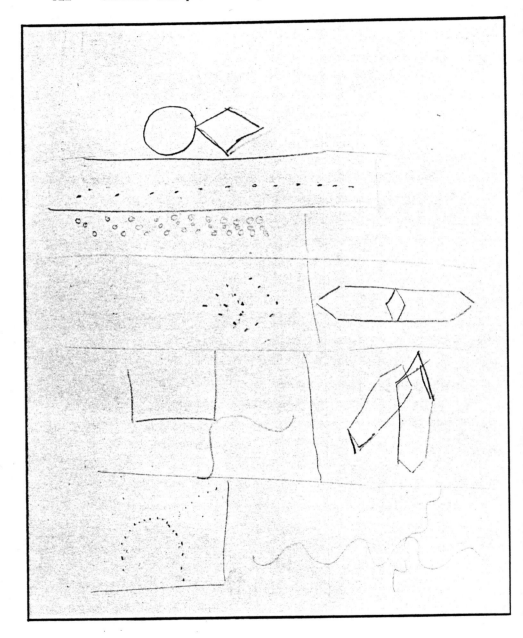

Case 02, Child Copy

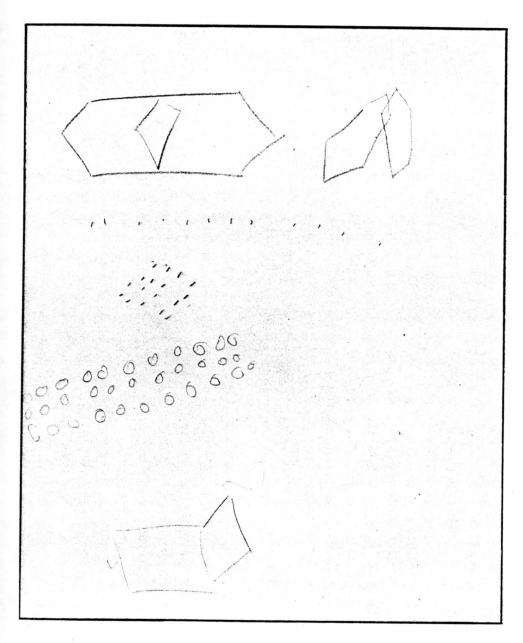

Case 02, Child Recall

other testing and diagnostic interviews. Presenting complaints were that he had serious difficulties with other children. Peer relations were marked by fighting, inability to compete and withdrawal. He either played with younger children or stayed by himself, spending much time reading. His behavior also tended to elicit ridicule from children his own age.

The sequence is orderly reflecting an age-appropriate capacity for intellectual organization. However, there is a suggestion of marked unconventionality. When he reached the bottom of the page he proceeded to place the designs in vertical order going from the bottom toward the top. This is a highly unusual direction which suggests a deviation from conventional ways of doing things. The number of populars in the Rorschach would give further information about his tendency to approach the world in an idiosyncratic manner. The F+% and analysis of the developmental level of percepts in the Rorschach would also give more detail about the adequacy of his reality testing and if his approach to the world is realistic as opposed to autistic.

The F+% should be at adult levels or higher for this age (F+%≥75) due to the increased use of intellectual defenses common in preadolescence and adolescence. If the F+% falls below adult levels there is reason to infer serious psychopathology or intracranial disturbance.

Drawing from the bottom of the page to the top is sometimes found with alienated individuals who have strong hostility and rebelliousness toward authority figures. Clinical data suggests there was serious chronic conflict between this boy and his parents which would tend to reinforce this inference from the direction of the reproductions.

Many difficulties appear in the angular figures. This includes lack of closure at joinings, workover of oblique angles and overruns and absorption (Fig. 8). One possible inference is that these errors reflect difficulties with the masculine role. His sexual identity may not be as firmly internalized as would be expected for a boy his age. The information that he was unable to compete with children in his own age group and the evidence of a high degree of overt hostility between himself and his father would tend to support this inference.

On an average, by eleven years of age most of the visual-motor development necessary for Bender reproductions at an adult level has been achieved. Although children do tend to be somewhat careless about closure, by eleven years of age more attention to accurate closure and joining is normally expected. This degree of closure deviation begins to be interpretable by this age and suggests fearfulness of bringing objects together. Often this characteristic is found where there is much fear and friction in interpersonal relations, an inference which was consistent with the presenting complaints.

Frequently children showing this difficulty will have a history of emotional deprivation. Clawson (1972) notes that children with closure errors have not had healthy and satisfying relationships with significant adults. Information from diagnostic interviews and a developmental history would help clarify this inference. The manner of handling color in the Rorschach would shed further light on how he has integrated emotion and cognition. M in the Rorschach would help clarify his conception of interpersonal roles. Often such children will have aggressive M's reflecting their difficulties in establishing and maintaining a role for themselves.

Much of the important information from this Bender protocol was contained in the general pervasive features discussed above. In this case analysis of the individual designs revealed somewhat less information than was true of the earlier cases. As with all clinical work and testing, each case is to a degree unique. A specific test or an aspect of a test may be very revealing for one person and yield only superficial information for another.

Figure A shows a circle that is drawn much more accurately than the square, reinforcing the earlier inference that he has anxiety around masculine identity and suggesting he perceives males as less adequate in some fashion than females or at least as somehow defective. He is more comfortable with feminine imagery. He may have identified more strongly with feminine roles. The other projective tests should shed more light on his sexual identity formation.

Figure 1 is essentially within expectation and suggests he has developed in some areas of his functioning to an age appropriate level. Figure 1 and Figure 2 both reflect some unevenness in maintaining the horizontal plane with a tendency to first gradually begin a counterclockwise rotation and then correct the design toward the end. By eleven years of age tendencies toward verticability are usually corrected which suggests that the counterclockwise deviations may represent a personality trend, i.e. a slight tendency toward acting out impulses which is quickly countered and controlled.

Figure 3 suggests that aggressive impulses may cause him some discomfort. He paused and broke the pattern, increasing the angulation toward the end of the design. If control of aggressive impulses is an area of conflict for him, then the boxes may very well represent a rigid and conscious attempt to contain unacceptable and poorly-integrated aggressive tendencies. The high degree of hostility reported in his familial and peer relations makes this hypothesis quite tenable.

Figure 4 has a size deviation. The rectangular subpart is exaggerated and the curved subpart has an increase in altitude. Oral dependency themes appear to be exaggerated and suggest he may very well have unresolved nurturant needs.

There is also a slight tendency toward separating the two subparts which are connected only by an overrun of a line from the rectangular subpart which reinforces the earlier inference of interpersonal anxiety. Moreover, dependency connotations sometimes evoked by this design would suggest that he tends to experience anxiety in relation to nurturing figures.

Figure 5 has a size distortion involving an exaggeration of the altitude of the base of the design. The increased curvature of Figure 4 and Figure 6 as well as Figure 5 suggests he tends to experience a strong emotional reaction to threatening impulses. The reaction to color and to dark shading in the Rorschach would help clarify the nature of his emotional reactivity. The slight clockwise rotation further suggests some depression which may be associated with pessimism about his ability to become adequate or assume the masculine role.

Figure 6 has been partially discussed. The emphasis in the reproductions on the left side of the design suggests a turning inward toward fantasy and a withdrawal from interaction with others; emphasis on top part of the design sometimes signals a tendency toward intellectualization. (These tendencies were confirmed in clinical observation and information from the home and school.)

Figure 7 has already been discussed in terms of angulation and joining deviations. Figure 8 has been partially discussed in terms of the joining difficulties. The absorption error of the inner diamond suggests that he may not always clearly observe boundaries between himself and others. There may be some tendency toward forming symbiotic relationships in which his identity blurs and blends with that of the other person. Evidence concerning identity formation should be sought from the projective techniques and other information about his development.

Analysis of Recall

The recall of seven figures makes it likely that his intelligence falls in at least the average range. As compared to the copy the most outstanding change on the recall was the omission of the boxes which suggests that part of what he was trying to control in the copy may have involved his feelings about taking orders, e.g. copying correctly on command. When left more to his own imagination he feels less constricted. In view of reports that he tends to withdraw from others this hypothesis seems quite tenable.

We have noticed that often children who show an improvement on the recall tend to have chronic hostility and oppositional tendencies toward authorities. Often this characteristic seems to be associated with a lack of a gratifying relationship with early dependency figures and suggests the importance of developmental information and an exploration of current family relationships as part of gaining an understanding of this child.

The use of space is more expansive, and Design 2 collides slightly with the edge of the page. One figure shows a contamination and resembles the square of Figure A with the circle replaced by another square. In general the form of the figures is less well preserved than in the copy and numerous rotations occur. The increase in errors reflects regression has occurred when the structure given by the stimulus cards was removed. When he is left to his own resources he becomes somewhat confused, expansive and mildly chaotic. The adequacy of his controls is very much in question as is also the degree of his reality testing and judgment.

The presence of a contamination strongly suggests serious ego deficiency. There is usually some evidence of confusion in thought processes with a tendency toward fluidity in thinking. Often a contamination reflects a schizophrenic process or intracranial dysfunction and is paralleled by tendencies toward bizarre or confused percepts in the Rorschach. His Rorschach responses did reveal some fluidity of boundaries and tendency toward an unrealistic and mildly bizarre blending of percepts and concepts similar to persons with a borderline psychotic adjustment.

The pervasive general tendencies reflected in the recall revealed much of the important information for this child similar to the copy. The individual designs added some detail not specifically apparent in the general features of the record.

Design 1 showed some tendency toward disorganization, and a clockwise rotation toward the end possibly signifying an increase in depressive reaction when he must rely more directly on himself. Design 2 was discussed previously except that it also shows an increase in tension and decrease in internal organization. The counterclockwise rotation could signify regression (similar to an age-appropriate design for a younger child) and acting out tendencies. Both regression and acting out of his emotions and aggressive impulses were evident in reports of his behavior. Figure 6 reveals further tendencies toward heightened reactivity and acting out as seen in increased angulation and counterclockwise rotation.

Figure 7 has a deviation in shape and a simplification. The dependent figure is made larger and more complete than the independent figure, suggesting that in his view dependency objects are inadequate to the demands of the dependent person in a relationship. In Figure 8 there is an exaggeration of the size of the figure suggesting further evidence that dependency themes are a source of concern and discomfort for him.

Integration

This young man presents the picture of a person who has ego impairments involving moderate confusion in thinking, conflict-ridden interpersonal relationships and strong tendencies to withdraw and regress under stress. He attempts to integrate and control himself primarily through the use of intellectual defenses which are brittle and soon give way under stress. These trends as seen in the Bender reproductions were well supported by other information from the test battery, from interviews and from clinical observations.

The specific source of the stress could not be identified from the Bender protocol. The strong feelings of inadequacy and unclear internalization of a masculine role may have been a part of the stress. Information available to us at the time this analysis was undertaken did not clearly identify the precipitating event for his regression. The examiner's notes provided reason to believe that the stresses of approaching adolescence and familial demands for achievement had combined to overwhelm the boy's tenuous resources for coping.

Comment

Some aspects of this record were quite unusual, especially the use of boxes which presents an idiosyncratic feature for interpretation. The majority of the inferences were based on the same considerations about normal and pathological performances in the Bender that have been demonstrated in previous cases.

In the present case information about child development entered the interpretive process in two distinct ways. First, the performance in the record as a whole and for each design was compared to normative information available from a variety of sources to determine whether a reproduction was at an age-appropriate level, regressed or precocious. This procedure led to hypotheses about deviations from expectancy and formulations about personality, dynamics and neurological substrate that might contribute to the observed deviations.

The second avenue by which information about child development contributed to the understanding came in the more extensive and speculative inferences that went beyond the specific interpretation of any single deviation. Hypotheses about the potential for family conflict, underlying emotional deprivation and the possible contribution of approaching adolescence fall into this second category of inferences.

Such inferences, although less closely tied to specific performances in the Bender, are not wild or purely theoretical. Understandings of normal and deviant child behavior derived from research and clinical experience make these inferences plausible working hypotheses to be verified or discarded in the light of additional information from other sources. Whether or not any specific inference is ultimately retained or rejected is of less importance in demonstrating the use of the Bender than the strategy of incorporating a developmental approach to Bender analysis when interpreting children's records.

CASE: 03

AGE: 14

SEX: Male

Analysis of Copy

The heavy pressure of the pencil evident in the dark lines of the reproductions immediately catches our attention. Line pressure is not a reliable indicator of conflict or personality disturbance with younger children because they tend to grasp the pencil more strongly as part of their efforts to achieve integration of visual attention with perceptual-motor coordination. However, this boy was in early adolescence, and when the strong pencil pressure occurs together with numerous other signs of disturbance (size deviations, irregular order, expansiveness, crowding of margins, angulation errors and joining errors) we are left with a strong impression that he is not functioning at an age-appropriate level.

The impression that some type of disturbance was present was consistent with the presenting complaints that led to the testing. This boy had a longstanding learning disability. Major problems included a tendency toward psychosomatic complaints, uncooperativeness in the classroom and high anxiety associated with achievement.

He spontaneously numbered the designs, suggesting an obsessive-compulsive defense. The reader should note that we will refer to the figures by their correct numbers, not by the subject's numbers. The position of the first and second design is uncommon insofar as they are closer to the margin than usual. This gives the overall impression of an individual who is somewhat anxious and fearful of others and feels the need to cling to

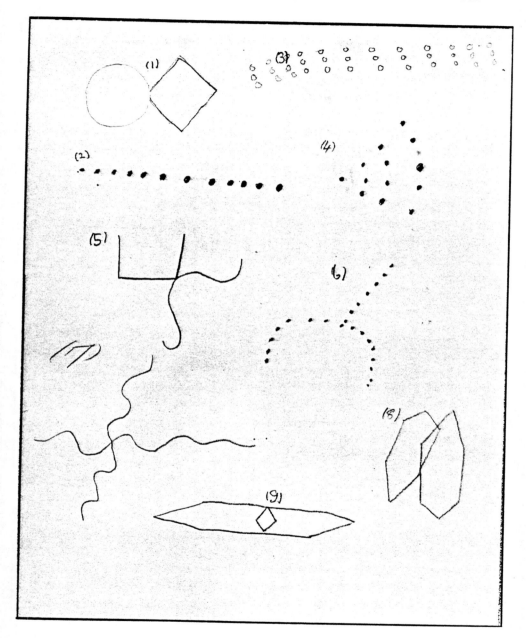

Case 03, Child Copy

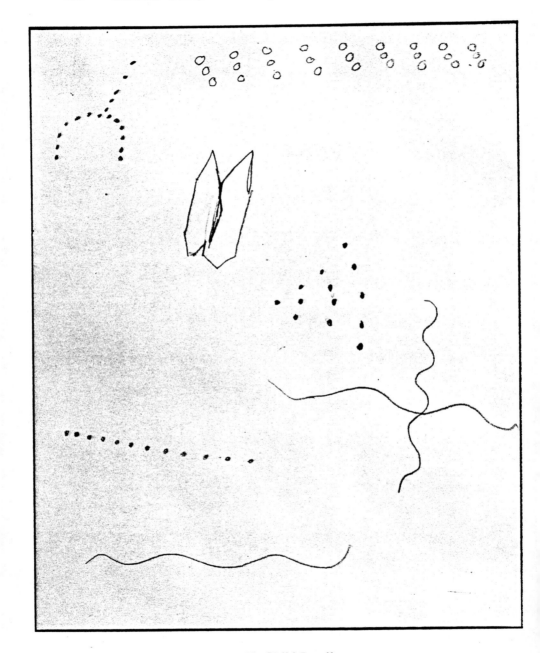

Case 03, Child Recall

something to gain security and structure. The tendency toward irregularity and disorganization is partially compensated by seeking external structure.

The numerous irregularities, the anxiety and the compulsivity seen in this Bender resemble the perceptual-motor deficiencies and compensatory efforts of older children who have had minimal brain dysfunction (MBD). Often these children display a complex of symptoms not unlike what this boy presented. Early perceptual-motor deficiencies make fine motor coordination difficult with the result that children with MBD cannot compete at an age-appropriate level.

The deficiency often becomes an ingrained part of their view of themselves. They feel inadequate and perceive themselves as failures, as they often have been, due to their visual-motor and cognitive deficiencies. Minimal brain dysfunction is a frequent basis for learning disabilities. Psychosomatic complaints are also frequent reflecting the vulnerability and anxiety such children feel. Compulsivity and the search for external guidelines such as using the margins or numbering are often the means by which they compensate for their inability to flexibly integrate and organize themselves. Since both this symptomatology and this manner of reproducing the Bender designs can also be the result of other anxieties and conflicts, a final diagnosis cannot be established from the Bender alone. The concurrence of the reported behavior patterns and the Bender protocol, however, establishes a strong hypothesis which would need to be carefully traced in the rest of the test battery and in the developmental history.

Figure A was drawn closer to the edge of the paper than is expected, suggesting some timidity and a tendency to cling to structure for support when faced with an achievement challenge. Figures 2, 3, 6 and 7 further reinforce this hypothesis. The light line pressure in Figure A suggests that as he starts out in a new situation he tends to draw back, indicating anxiety and self-doubt. A joining error of absorption occurred, indicating some problems exist concerning accurate perception of boundaries between objects. Figure 7 and Figure 8 and the crossover point in Figure 6 also reveal some joining errors, suggesting that he is moderately sensitive to relationships between people and may have some difficulties in establishing smooth contacts. Often children showing this difficulty are fearful of interpersonal relationships. At times this sensitivity will also be seen in a relatively high picture completion subtest in the Wechsler Intelligence Scale for Children. The absorption also connotes that he may not have established as firm an individual identity as would be expected for his age.

An alternative plausible hypothesis for the errors of closure is maturational lag similar to that seen in children who have minimal brain dysfunction. Younger children are often careless about closure of lines and joinings of parts. A younger mental age, i.e. neurological lag, could account for this tendency in a child this age who would otherwise be expected to perform at a more mature level.

Figure 1 has an enlargement of dots often found where there are internal tensions which do not have adequate channels for expression. The dots grow progressively larger, suggesting the longer he stays with a task demanding concentrated attention, the greater the difficulty he experiences in controlling himself. There is a moderate potential for acting out and poor frustration tolerance. The manner of coping with color and dark shading in the Rorschach would give further information on this hypothesis.

The slight downward rotation may be too small to interpret. If it is meaningful it suggests some tendency to dampen or inhibit affect. Figure 6 suggests this hypothesis is plausible. He tends to be moderately unresponsive to his own emotions and tends to deny or flatten the emotional stimulation emanating from others. Analysis of the use of color in the Rorschach would clarify this hypothesis. Often with such indications in the Bender we have noticed the child will tend to avoid meaningful interpretations of color and have a very low Sum C in the Rorschach, indicating flatness of affect and tendencies toward acting out emotions. The presenting complaint of psychosomatic symptoms is consistent with the hypothesis that his anxiety and emotions are poorly integrated with his personality and cognition.

Figure 2 is slightly rotated counterclockwise. Vertical rotation in Figure 2 is common before age ten and in this case is a further indication of the presence of immaturity of functioning. A tendency to act out emotions and impulses is sometimes associated with counterclockwise rotations. He corrected the rotation in time to avoid a collision with the edge of the page, suggesting that reality testing and foresight are intact. He failed to plan ahead adequately, however, to the degree that he had to make a last minute adjustment in order to avoid a collision. His foresight and planning are like that of a younger child who largely selects spaces rather than proceeds by an organized plan.

Figure 3 shows the same treatment of the dots as Figure 1 with the same interpretation applying. A simplification occurred with too few dots and the height of the figure was increased. Size distortions also occurred in Figures A, 4, 5 and 6 with some figures expanded and others reduced. Such variability is often found with children who have an emotional disturbance, although the specific details of the disturbance are not necessarily indicated. Variability in size often occurs with acting out children who have poor impulse control and capacity for delay. The combination of size distortions and simplification in Figure 3 suggests that he has a moderate degree of conflict concerning the control or expression of aggressive impulses.

Content of the other projective devices might clarify this thesis. The reported symptomatology included references to anxiety about achievement. One dynamic often found in underachievement is fear of self-assertion which would be consistent with the hypothesis that he has conflicts concerning modulating and expressing aggression.

Figure 4 reveals a slight increase in the size of the square subpart and the altitude of the curves, suggesting either a continuation of the mild expansive trend seen in Figure 3 or a reaction to the symbolic connotations of Figure 4. If he was reacting to the dependency symbolism thought to be aroused by this figure, it would suggest that oral dependency themes are a concern for him. The examiner's notes did suggest a passive-dependent attitude was typical of his behavior during testing.

Figure 5 continues the expansive trend and also shows simplification. He tends to shorten the task by leaving out some of the dots, similar to his treatment of Figure 3. The expansiveness suggests some chronic tendency toward overreaction to emotional stimulation and the possibility that he has difficulty controlling himself. Since the form of the figure is retained it is likely that his efforts to control his impulses do work moderately well.

The increased size of Figure 5 may also reflect concerns about the masculine role and suggests he may feel some discomfort over internalizing a masculine identity. The sketching and size increase in Figure A further reinforces the hypothesis of some conflict and anxiety concerning masculine imagery.

The slight clockwise rotation of Figure 5 suggests some tendency to flatten affect at times. The decrease in the altitude of the sine waves in Figure 6 further supports the inference of some tendency to flatten affect and to avoid emotional stimulation. Some impoverishment of impulses and emotions is often a concomitant of reducing the curved aspects of the designs. The shakiness of line quality at the crossover point in Figure 6 suggests he has anxiety associated with interpersonal interactions.

Figure 7 shows some upward displacement of the left subpart and a change in angulation at the top of the right subpart. A similar loss of angulation (simplification) is seen in Figure 8. As in the earlier designs (Figs. 3 and 5), the simplifications suggest a regressive trend, implying immaturity in his ability to sustain goal-directed, concentrated effort. Often impulse delay and capacity for sustaining goal-directed attention is deficient in children who simplify this many designs.

Either structural (organic) or functional impairments can cause simplifications. The many signs of a variety of small errors seen in this boy's protocol suggest a pervasive incompletely-compensated lag in perceptual motor functioning. A developmental analysis of Rorschach percepts would help clarify the organic versus the emotional basis of these deviations. The one factor that is clear is that he has a moderate degree of impairment in his functioning beyond what would be expected for his age. This is very commonly seen in the protocols of children with learning disabilities.

Analysis of Recall

The recall of six figures suggests that mental deficiency is not likely to be the basis of the observed deviations seen in the copy. The Wechsler Intelligence Scale for Children and estimates of intelligence made from the Thematic Apperception Test and the Rorschach would help clarify his level of intellectual functioning.

Simplification occurs in all but Figure 1, and four of the six figures hug the margins, suggesting that when he is left to his own resources he becomes increasingly anxious and tends to constrict and distort. He would very likely function more effectively in a structured situation. Often children with learning disabilities who show a reaction to being left on their own require more individual attention in the classroom. The complaints about his lack of achievement and uncooperativeness should be explored with the teachers to see if he responds more favorably to individualized supportive attention.

Design 1 shows tension in the blackened dots and has a mild downward rotation, suggesting a flattening of affect and depressiveness when he faces threatening situations. Figure 6 also shows a slight downward rotation and flattening of the curves, but the vertical subpart is rotated counterclockwise, suggesting a conflict between tendencies to act out his impulses and tendencies to constrict and inhibit himself. Figure 3 shows a similar flattening of angulation, suggesting that he tends to inhibit his aggressive impulses. Figure 6 was begun, abandoned and finally completed, suggesting self-doubt in regard to the expression of spontaneous emotion.

Altogether these contradictory signs suggest that he has conflicts and ambivalence about how to modulate or express his emotions and impulses. He acts first one way and then another which makes his actions difficult to predict. Such variability is often found where there has been a history of unstable emotional socialization. Analysis of shading and color responses in the Rorschach would shed further light on his ambivalence and chaotic defensive pattern.

Integration

This young man presents the picture of a person with pervasive mild tendencies to regress under stress. It also appears that he must seek external support and guidance in order to function up to his potential. In many ways he resembles children who have had some minimal brain dysfunction and who, through maturation and learning, have compensated for the impairments.

Whether there is a neurological substrate or primarily functional basis it is clear from the Bender protocol that his functioning is not up to age level. He shows many signs of disturbance, inner tensions, ambivalence about emotional expression and a chaotic defensive system which makes him erratic and puzzling. He often fails where performance in other aspects of the Bender would suggest he has the capability to succeed. He sometimes tries to cope and adapt by inhibiting himself, and at other times he acts out on his impulses. His level of functioning shows increased regressiveness when he must depend on his own resources. Whether the basis for the erratic performance is a neurological deficiency or his personality and dynamics, it is clear that there is unevenness in development and/or functioning which would usually also be seen in the intelligence test profile and in the other projective devices. Regression and erratic functioning are often found with children who have learning disabilities.

Comment

This record presented the opportunity to see how the Bender can reflect many of the patterns of functioning in an adolescent that can be associated with learning disabilities. The Bender has been found in clinical work and in diagnostic testing to reflect many aspects of development, organicity and personality which can affect a person's learning capacity in a variety of ways.

The topic of learning disabilities is far too complex and extensive to be discussed here. We only wish to point out that many of the capacities related to formal learning are also required for adequate reproduction of the Bender designs. The relationship between deviations in the Bender and learning disabilities is far from simple or straightforward. In many cases the neurological and/or personality variables associated with a given learning disability are also reflected in Bender reproductions. Of course such association does not necessarily imply that one causes the other. Rather, both the Bender and formal learning require certain complexes of capacities and motivations. Impairments in these capacities can simultaneously be reflected in impairments in functioning in the classroom situation and in the Bender reproductions.

In the present case the erratic quality of the boy's performance, his difficulties in modulating his emotions, his lack of self-confidence and his need to cling to someone or something were inferred from his Bender reproductions. They were also evident in his behavior and were partly responsible for his inability to profit from the classroom experience. We find it is the exception rather than the rule to find a child who has a clearly identified learning disability and a fully age-appropriate Bender protocol.

APPENDIX

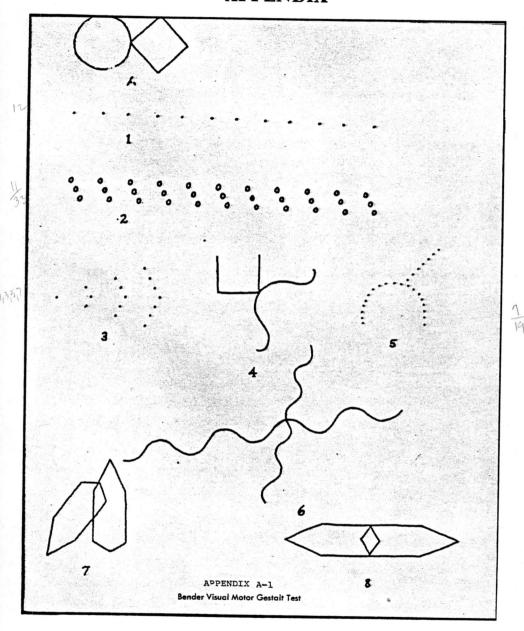

APPENDIX A-1
Bender Visual Motor Gestalt Test

141

	Figure A.	Figure 1.	Figure 2.	Figure 3.	Figure 4.	Figure 5.	Figure 6.	Figure 7.	Figure 8.
Adult.	100%	25%	100%	100%	100%	100%	100%	100%	100%
11 yrs.	95%	95%	65%	60%	95%	90%	70%	75%	90%
10 yrs.	90%	90%	60%	60%	80%	80%	60%	60%	90%
9 yrs.	80%	75%	60%	70%	80%	70%	80%	65%	70%
8 yrs.	75%	75%	75%	60%	80%	65%	70%	65%	65%
7 yrs.	75%	75%	70%	60%	75%	65%	60%	65%	60%
6 yrs.	75%	75%	60%	80%	75%	60%	60%	60%	75%
5 yrs.	85%	85%	60%	80%	70%	60%	60%	60%	75%
4 yrs.	90%	85%	75%	80%	70%	60%	65%	60%	60%
3 yrs.	------------- Scribbling -------------								

APPENDIX A-2

Maturational Norms

REFERENCES

Ackerman, Peggy T., Peters, John E., and Dykman, Roscoe A.: Children with specific learning disabilities: Bender Gestalt test findings and other signs. *J Learn Disabil, 4*(8):437-446, 1971.

Armstrong, R. G.: A re-evaluation of copied and recalled Bender Gestalt reproductions. *J Projective Tech Pers Assess, 29:*134-139, 1965.

Armstrong, R. G., and Hauck, P. A.: Correlates of the Bender Gestalt scores in children. *J Psychol Studies, 11:*153-158, 1960.

Bain, Bruce: Further information on the Bender Gestalt as a group test for screening school children. *Percept Motor Skills, 33*(3-P+2):1204, 1971.

Bender, L.: *Instructions for Use of the Visual Motor Gestalt Test.* New York, American Orthopsychiatric Association, 1946.

Bender, L.: *A Visual Motor Gestalt Test and its Clinical Use.* American Orthopsychiatric Association, Research Monograph No. 3, New York, American Orthopsychiatric Association, 1938.

Bender, L.: Use of the Visual Motor Gestalt Test in the diagnosis of learning disabilities. *J Spec Ed, 4*(1):29-39, 1970.

Clawson, Eileen: *The Bender Visual Motor Gestalt Test for Children.* Los Angeles, Western Psychological Services, 1962.

Cleary, T. Anne, Humphreys, Lloyd G., Kendrick, S. A., and Wesman, Alexander: Educational uses of tests with disadvantaged students. *Am Psychol, 30,* 1975.

Coy, Michael N.: The Bender Visual Motor Gestalt Test as a predictor of academic achievement. *J Learn Disabil, 7*(5):317-319, 1974.

Cronbach, Lee J.: Five decades of public controversy over mental testing. *Am Psychol, 30*(1):1-14, 1975.

Eaves, L. C., Kendall, D. C., and Crichton, J. U.: The early detection of minimal brain dysfunction. *J Learn Disabil, 5*(8):454-462, 1972.

Farmer, Rae H.: Functional changes during early weeks of abstinence, measured by the Bender Gestalt. *Q J Studies Alcohol, 34*(3-Part A):786-796, 1973.

Fiedler, Miriam F., and Schmidt, Ellen P.: Sex differences in Bender Gestalt drawings of seven-year-old children. *Perceptual and Motor Skills, 29*(3):753-754, 1969.

Fuller, J. B., and Chagnon, G.: Factors influencing rotation in the Bender Gestalt performance of children. *J Proj Tech, 26:*36-46, 1962.

Garron, D. C., and Cheifetz, D. I.: Comment of Bender Gestalt discernment of organic pathology. *Psychol Bull, 63:*197-200, 1965.

Gavales, D., and Millon, T.: Comparison of reproduction and recall size deviations in the Bender Gestalt as measures of anxiety. *J Clin Psychol*, *16*:278-280, 1960.

Gravitz, Herbert L.: Examiner expectance effects in psychological assessment: The Bender Visual Motor Gestalt Test. *Dissertation Abstracts International*, *30*(11-B):5238, 1970.

Gravitz, Herbert L., and Handler, Leonard: Effects of different modes of administration on the Bender Visual Motor Gestalt Test. *J Consult Clin Psychol*, *32*(3):276-279, 1968.

Griffith, R. M., and Taylor, V. H.: Bender Gestalt figure rotations: A stimulus factor. *J Consult Psychol*, *25*:89-90, 1961.

Griffith, R. M., and Taylor, V. H.: Incidence of Bender Gestalt figure rotations. *J Consult Psychol*, *24*:189-190, 1960.

Hain, J. D.: The Bender Gestalt Test: A scoring method for identifying brain damage. *J Consult Psychol*, *28*:34-40, 1964.

Hinsie, Leland E., and Campbell, Robert J.: *Psychiatric Dictionary*. New York, Oxford U Pr, 1970.

Hutt, Max L.: *The Hutt Adaptation of the Bender Gestalt Test*. New York, Grune, 1960.

Hutt, Max L., and Gibby, Robert Gwyn: *An Atlas for the Hutt Adaptation of the Bender Gestalt Test*. New York, Grune, 1970.

Hutt, Max L., and Miller, Lawrence J.: Further studies of a measure of adience-abience: Reliability. *J Pers Assess*, *39*(2):123-128, 1975.

Kalil, Albert J.: A reliability study of the Bender Visual Motor Gestalt Test when administered and scored under special conditions. *Dissertation Abstracts International*, *30*(60-A):2378, 1969.

Kaspar, Joseph C., and Lampel, Anita K.: Interrater reliability for scoring the Bender Gestalt using the Koppitz method. *Percept Motor Skills*, *34*(3):765, 1972.

Koegh, B. K., and Smith, C. E.: Group techniques and proposed scoring system for the Bender Gestalt Test with children. *J Clin Psychol*, *17*:172, 1961.

Kerr, Andrew S.: Determinants of performance of the Bender Gestalt Test in Raven's Progressive Matrices (1947) Test. *J Learn Disabil*, *5*(4):219-221, 1972.

Killian, L. R.: WISC, Illinois Test of Psycholinguistic Abilities, and Bender Visual-Motor Gestalt Test performance of Spanish-American kindergarten and firstgrade school children. *J Consult Clin Psychol*, *37*(1):38, 1971.

Koppitz, Elizabeth M.: *The Bender Gestalt Test with the Human Figure Drawing Test for Young Children*. State of Ohio, Department of Education, 1972.

Koppitz, E. M.: The Bender Gestalt Test for Children: A normative study. *J Clin Psychol*, *16*:432-435, 1960.

Koppitz, E. M.: *The Bender Gestalt Test for Young Children*. New York, Grune, 1964.

Kramer, E., and Fenwick, J.: Differential diagnosis with the Bender Gestalt Test. *J Proj Tech Pers Assess, 30:*59-61, 1966.

Lambert, Nadine M.: An evaluation of scoring categories applicable to children's performance on the Bender Visual Motor Gestalt Test. *Psychol Schools,* 7(3):275-287, 1970.

Lambert, Nadine M.: An item analysis and validity investigation of Bender Visual Motor Gestalt Test items. *Psychol in the Schools,* 8(1):78-85, 1971.

Lerner, Edna A.: *The Projective Use of the Bender Gestalt.* Springfield, Thomas, 1972.

Matranga, James T., Jensen, Diana E., and Prandonic, Joques R.: Bender Gestalt protocols of adult Negro male offenders: Normative data. *Percept Motor Skills,* 35(1):101-102, 1972.

Miller, Lawrence J., and Hutt, Max L.: Psychopathology scale of the Hutt Adaptation of the Bender Gestalt Test: Reliability. *J Pers Assess,* 39(2):129, 1975.

Mosher, D. L., and Smith, J. P.: The usefulness of two scoring systems for the Bender Gestalt Test for identifying brain damage. *J Consult Psychol,* 29:530-536, 1965.

Nussbaum, K., Shoffer, J. W., and Schneidmuhl, A. M.: Psychological assessment in the social security program of disability insurance. *Am Psychol,* 24(9):869-872, 1969.

Parsons, Lowell B., McLeroy, Nancy, and Wright, Logan: Validity of Koppitz's developmental score as a measure of organicity. *Percept Motor Skills,* 33(3-P+1):1013-1014, 1971.

Pope, Peggy, and Snyder, Robert T.: Modification of selected Bender designs and interpretation of the first grader's visual perceptual maturation with implications for Gestalt theory. *Percept Motor Skills,* 30(1):263-367, 1970.

Rhodes, Jon G.: A comparative study of individually and group administered Visual Motor Gestalt Test as related to academic achievement. *Dissertation Abstracts International,* 33(6-A):2792, 1972.

Savastano, Helena, and deDomini, Juliana: The Visual Motor Gestalt Test in adults: Preliminary study. *Revista de Psicologia Normal e Patologica,* 16(3-4):221, 1970.

Schafer, Roy: *Psychoanalytic Interpretation in Rorschach Testing.* New York, Grune, 1954.

Schulberg, H. C., and Tolor, A.: The use of the Bender Gestalt Test in clinical practice. *J Proj Tech,* 25:347-351, 1961.

Smith, Donald C., and Martin, Robert A.: Use of learning cues with the Bender Visual Motor Gestalt Test in screening children with neurological impairment. *J Consult Psychol,* 31(2):205, 1967.

Snyder, Robert T., Holowenzak, Stephen P., and Hoffman, Norma: A cross-cultural item-analysis of Bender Gestalt protocols administered to ghetto and suburban children. *Percept Motor Skills,* 33(3-P+1):791-796, 1971.

Sternberg, D., and Levine, A.: An indicator of suicidal ideation on the Bender Visual Motor Gestalt Test. *J Proj Tech Pers Assess,* 29:377-379, 1965.

Stoer, L., Corotto, L. V., and Curnutt, R. H.: The role of visual perception in reproduction of Bender Gestalt designs. *J Proj Tech Pers Assess, 29*:473-478, 1965.

Story, R. I.: The revised Bender Gestalt Test and male alcoholics. *J Proj Tech, 24*:186, 1960.

Taylor, Henry D., and Thweath, Roger C.: Cross cultural developmental performance of Navajo children on the Bender Gestalt Test. *Percept Motor Skills, 35*(1):307-309, 1972.

Tolor, A., and Schulberg, H.: *An Evaluation of the Bender Gestalt Test.* Springfield, Thomas, 1963.

Tolor, A.: The "meaning" of the Bender Gestalt Test designs: a study in the use of the semantic differential. *J Proj Tech, 24*:433-438, 1960.

Ward, William J.: A comparison of distortion scores on the Bender Visual Motor Gestalt Test using circular and rectangular protocol sheets. *Dissertation Abstracts International, 30*(5-A):1883, 1969.

Welsher, Doris W., Wessel, Kenneth W., Mellits, E. David, and Hardy, Janet B.: The Bender Gestalt test as an indicator of neurological impairment in young innercity children. *Percept Motor Skills, 38*(3-P+1):899-910, 1974.

Willis, Diane J., and Pishkin, Vladimir: Perceptual-motor performance on the Vane and Bender tests as related to two socio-economic classes and ages. *Percept Motor Skills, 38*(3-P+1):883-890, 1974.